The Wire Mother
Monkey Chronicles

The Wire Mother Monkey Chronicles

Dan Dewey

To order additional copies of this book, contact:
Xlibris Corporation
1-888-795-4274
www.Xlibris.com
Orders@Xlibris.com
104859

CONTENTS

HARLOW'S SURROGATE MOTHER EXPERIMENT

Harry Frederick Harlow (October 31, 1905-December 6, 1981) was an American psychologist best known for his maternal-separation and social isolation experiments on rhesus monkeys, which demonstrated the importance of tangible affection in social and cognitive development.

In a well-known series of experiments conducted between 1957 and 1963, Harlow removed baby rhesus monkeys from their mothers, and offered them a choice between two surrogate mothers, one made of terrycloth, the other of wire.

Harlow's interpretation of this behavior, which is still widely accepted, was that lack of contact comfort was psychologically stressful to the monkeys.

The importance of these findings is that they contradicted both the then common pedagogic advice of limiting or avoiding bodily contact in an attempt to avoid spoiling children and the insistence of the then dominant behaviorist school of psychology that emotions were negligible.

Partial and total isolation of infant monkeys

From around 1960 onwards, Harlow and his students began publishing their observations on the effects of partial and total social isolation. Partial isolation involved raising monkeys in bare wire cages that allowed them to see, smell, and hear other monkeys, but provided no opportunity for physical contact. Total social isolation involved rearing monkeys in isolation chambers that precluded any and all contact with other monkeys.

lack of contact comfort was psychologically stressful to the monkeys.

Harlow et al. reported that partial isolation resulted in various abnormalities such as blank staring, stereotyped repetitive circling in their cages, and self-mutilation. These monkeys were then observed in various settings. Some of the monkeys remained in solitary confinement for 15 years.

In the total isolation experiments baby monkeys would be left alone for three, six, 12, or 24 months of "total social deprivation." The experiments produced monkeys that were severely psychologically disturbed.

Critics of Harlow's research have observed that clinging is a matter of survival in young rhesus monkeys, but not in humans, and have suggested that his conclusions, when applied to humans, overestimate the importance of contact comfort and underestimate the importance of nursing. Harlow's enduring legacy then, reinforced the importance of emotional support, affection, and love in the development of children

Recently, my mother stressed to me that I myself was nursed at least as she apologized for "the then common pedagogic advice of limiting or avoiding bodily contact" that she was given.

THE BROOKLYN BOMBER

"The true test of civilization is, not the census, nor the size of the cities, |
nor the crops,—no, but the kind of man the country turns out."

Ralph Waldo Emerson

Some of us are musicians, some athletes, and some warriors, nurturers, gadflies . . . I am a loner and like Jefferson, wouldn't go to Heaven if the journey required going in a group. According to the Myers/Brigs Personality Inventory only 1% of the population thinks like I do which gives me pause to shudder—while you reflect on Ortega's, "Anybody who is not like everybody, who does not think like everybody runs the risk of being eliminated. (Revolt of the Masses.)

Life for a two year old is a blast of awareness. Colors. The dry crinkly smell of leaves. Is there a psychologist alive who has never read that, "The baby, assaulted by eye, ears, nose, skin and entrails at once, feels it all as one great blooming, buzzing confusion"? Probably not, you see, psychologists are fed as much if not more bullshit than the rest of us. Perception is active, exploratory and motivated even in the two day old infant (Gibson, 1987). Meaning, even as infants, our perceptions are not pure chaos, ala Wm. James. Rather, early perception is a search for order almost from day one.

Flatbush, the Great State of Brooklyn. Home. I was born there. A place which still glows of open-air markets colorful produce. Autumn leaf piles covering young tangled limbs. Christmas Time.

My father left home then, He was always in and out of jail, until one day he stopped coming home and that was the end of his record. On our memory side anyway. 78 rpm. Ziiiiip. I never asked Frederick, Jr. if he remembered dear old dad. I didn't recollect anything but shadows. Not surprising since Mommy told me that Grandma had told her never to touch or hold us except for changing our diapers so as not to spoil us. Mommy also said, much later, father was about to kill us and my brother changed his name one day forever, so maybe he did remember something. I didn't want to know. I had enough to deal with in the here and now.

Mommy got a job and fled to Grandma who did not spare the rod, the wall, the strap or hairbrush in keeping my brother and I civilized and I have the scars to prove it. I'm not sure what was being communicated, but I guess we were civilized. (Acquiring brain lesions can do that?) I was thrifty, kind, clean, reverent, and learned to not be seen or heard. Well, scratch reverent. All I knew at the time was the Roman Catholic Church—an aerobic exercise for sitting and standing at the sound of a bell. And who could understand Latin? If I could have, I still would not have understood that all the great world religions supposedly represented and expressed Man's public concern with his existence. As far as I knew, religion was about not going to hell and everyone was going to hell except for "good" Roman Catholics who refused to die. All I wanted from God was a bicycle.

I loved to spend my time going through the Park; under bushes, around trees, benches, rocks, bags, trashcans. Bottles all over. Big ones were worth 5 cents, little ones—1 cent. There wasn't much competition with everyone else in school so soon I was off to the grocery store running pell-mell, inevitably into their Mountain of Returns, always anxious they had so many—mine wouldn't be taken, not understanding Economics then. The guns and butter science. Although I did know which side the butter was on and which way it usually fell made me more of a pessimist than an optimist. (The optimist sees the water at the watering hole, period, while the pessimist looks for the tiger tracks around it first.) I know more about butter and lots about guns now, as the economists do, yet if you stretched all their theories out in a line—they wouldn't reach a conclusion. In other words, there is no exit to any Absolute truths from within the Castle of Economics or Science for that matter.

A dollar of bottles did mean a strawberry shortcake with honest to goodness real whipped cream. (A kid had to eat the whole thing at once in the summer and I could handle it.) A dollar also meant a Dinky toy tank. Awesome detail. Impregnable, with real linked-metal tracks. They were on my side. Even the German ones.

Public school was iron-grated stairs teeming with civilized people. At least they wore clothes and spoke cryptic sounds. An initiation into the halls of reductionistic learning strategy. I bombed out of second grade twice. My brother was bombed with parts of a public works project. I was frozen between running and staying, but thawed out and abandoned him. I started to bomb windows and the English language with loose objects and F words somewhere between Brooklyn and Newark, N.J. This did not please my Grandma, who had filled our new home again with boarders. Aha! Dollars equal a room. More learning in Economics. Mommy taught us a lesson in priorities. She found a way to get us to Hope Farm after her mother demonstrated her Germanic behavior control by grabbing my brother's hair and banging his head into the wall. My brother and I bombed out of Newark, the mosquito capital, with the help of the NYC Children's Court. Thank you Mommy.

Hope Farm. A land with no empty bottles. No returns. Dormitories the far side of civilization. Counting the new cries of homesickness—I was always ambivalent about new kids. I felt their pain and wished they would bite the bullet. For me, the emptiness of Visitor's Day was louder than the inner crumbling of belonging. I was marooned. That was my truth at the time. Awareness has a way of broadening itself. The truth is, we were abandoned. I felt more like marooned. Like the Family ship hit the rocks and here I was—strange little kid in a stranger land.

Marcy Cottage

There was no hope at the Farm for my brother. He got Rheumatic fever and then, Diabetes, so They bussed him off to a place with medical stuff.

We used to fight most times anyway so it was probably O.K. that we never saw much of each other after that. I was a bright kid. They gave me an I.Q. test and put me in the fourth grade.

Living in the dorms was hard if you wanted to be alone some of the time. Especially in the morning. Getting a good toilet or sink meant interpersonal relationships. For a long time I only lasted a few minutes after wake-up before one of my molecules set everything to boil. (And like the Brownian Movement—I never knew which molecule would go first.) I didn't even know what a molecule was. There was always some kid willing to check, even my brother. The older we got the less the other kids checked. We realized that we were all on the same island and by the grace of God and reaching 18, we would leave.

Tony V-neck was my best friend from the Marcy dorms. One growth spurt from Plum, where the real little shits still peed in their pants. Tony wore white socks and played the game. He even fell in love with the minister's daughter. (She was "straight" in more ways then vertical.) Tony said falling in love was like a bolt of lightening. We were eleven. I imagined a bolt on a clear blue day, but didn't see the flash. Tony was sure different. Anyway, Tony got religious and talked about grace and Jesus, but he stilled played good football.

I thought I was a white Anglo Saxon Protestant (WASP) then even though I had been baptized Roman Catholic to avoid Limbo. I was saved, apparently from Catholicism, through Episcopal communion and the touch of a Bishop. I could now eat the essence of Jesus Christ's flesh. That's how much I understood attending Episcopal confirmation classes in exchange for being allowed to play ball later.

I hated wasps. When they stung me my body would swell up far from the teeny puncture. I thought I was allergic to my own kind. Some of my parts are German too (maternal) and, ironically, I later helped burn children—and rice paddies, straw huts, men, women, water buffalo, and the enemy de jour of our leaders, (mostly shorter, browner and flatter nosed peoples) while helping to reduce villages to rubble, then to debris, then to dust and finally, to nothing.

I used to smash wasps with anything I could find, usually the newspaper. "Smashed with the Truth" (that's fit to print), those wasps were forever bent.

I hope they didn't feel anything—their separated parts still functioning, just like us animal wasps. We have a million parts all functioning separately, the less tangible, the least control. ID, Ego, hands, stomach, head, heart, feet. No part is in total control. Sometimes parts get stung by stinging parts—just like our bug cousins. Same here. I've hurt myself for years, thinking someone was trying to smash me with a newspaper. Truth. Theory. Rules. I had my own mental notes to hit myself with.

I used to think. Actually, after I started to think, I dropped the "P" (for the wrong reason) and became a "WAS". This felt more appropriate. I needed to get God out of this mess. I was trying to buy into the Program. I never got in. I never dropped out. I just continually stung myself in disbelief.

"Why did you run away?" staff wants to know.

Because I'm 12 now and hungrier doesn't wash. They think I did it on purpose to get them in trouble, like I had a plan or something. Some plan—hitchhike 10 miles to the Dover Plains train, try to evade conductor moving between cars until Grand Central Station, but he usually cornered you, run across street to get a sandwich at Horn and Hardots Automat, and try to get back before the State Police returned me.

Although we claim that we're conscious, we have scarcely a clue about what's happening in our brains. E.g. we haven't the faintest notion how ideas are constructed or how words are chosen. Instead we say, "Something just occurred to me!" or "We have free-will"—not recognizing that we hardly know the reasons for most of our choices. (Minsky, 1993). Heck, we can now take apart the 3 lb. brain bundle piece by piece, map the neurotransmitters, test each component, marvel at the more than 100 trillion connections, but we can't get close to explaining how all the individual parts work in concert to produce consciousness (McAuliffe, circa 1990.) Not through "reductionism" anyway.

Staff were still out there vibrating air. "Don't roll your eyes when I'm talking to you."

I don't think I handled being singled out that well. It's really weird to feel alone, estranged, separate, whatever, and then be the focus of some moral train wreck or something. Well, I was guilty of breaking some adult rule, so to the other kids I was just doomed—not a wimp. To myself, running was not a mortal sin. I was used to the mortal one anyway—we are born into it, which necessitates aerobics every Sunday. And Wednesday morning, I guess to prevent Sunday from wearing off.

I forget what the punishment was, but I remember that when you swim "up river"—you swim it alone. Your dorm mates, blank faced strangers on the bank mutely staring from a personal relief they hadn't screwed up. Collective punishment wasn't that bad. On an individual basis though, I literally jumped out of my skin in shock. (A positive adaptive mechanism of dissociation with rigor mortis.) This is because we do not merely get disturbed from relationships with parents or culture, as psychoanalysis alleges, nor do we mainly get upset at environmental conditions like poverty and war; as many psychotherapists insist; No, we make ourselves upset (Ellis, 1992).

I liked Tony a lot. He was happy in his beliefs. We were friends who got away from the Farm once in a great while to his Mom's in Brooklyn, ostensibly to "get away" but really to experience the heights of pubescent decadence—42nd Street & Times Square. Tony's Mom was cool though, she was poor as dirt and had to work while we were there, but she always had a couple of dollars for us. I liked her. Civilization. Movies to the 10th power. We picked a great adventure—a pedophile Tie and Jacket authority figure grabbed my leg half-way through. Shit. I switched seats with Tony and never said a word. (I'm sorry Tony.) I have no idea what the movie was and I sure as Hell don't know who is responsible here.

I had my own bed, clothes locker and an old AM radio without a cover that my Grandfather had given me. On receipt he said, "Take care of yourself Danny." Not—I love you—I'll take care of you, but more like, 'You are responsible for your own existence Danny—I can't be and God doesn't want to be.' I forgot who was responsible for what, but loved the glowing vacuum tubes. I got to like most of the kids too. They glowed on me, I was basically happy in the context of aching.

Larry was a Jew at the Farm. I called him "Hebe" plenty of times. He was smaller than I was. I think I would have understood Rabbi Heschel then when he said, "The degree to which one is sensitive to other people's suffering, to another's humanity, is the index of one's own humanity." Mark Twain's Devil in The Mysterious Stranger pretty much said the same thing backwards. I.E. The degree to which a person is insensitive to the suffering of mankind is the degree of their inhumanity. I knew this, when I stopped calling Larry names, before I forgot.

Excitement? We made the galvanized pipe cannons out of matches, charcoal and cotton to shoot walls and dug underground forts to smoke staff's cigarette butts. Sometimes it was necessary to make a foray to Gate House for bicycle parts. Spooning peas like a rocket onto the dinning hall ceiling was cool too, especially if you had institutional peas. Most kids would eat anything. Did you ever go on an Easter egg hunt and get sick? I did. Jelly beans. That's all They had one year at the Farm. Up the banisters, 'top of the doors, in the dormitories, down the stairs, in the kitchen, dining hall, foyers and living rooms. Some kid said, he found a green one behind a toilet. Nobody looked further. End of excitement.

To belong at the Farm meant playing football too. On the field and off. I hated football, at least the hitting part. If you wanted to belong you played in the Program. I played but didn't like the Program. Now Donny, my longest dorm brother, loved the Program and like most of us, came from deep within the City where those little White Castle hamburgers lived. At 13, he had never touched a football or met so much grass in one place. But he wanted to play with a fever. That's all he talked about off the bus—i.e. whether we played football. He never once looked for the Exit sign. Donny seemed predestined to succeed. As if basking in some Divine Grace; Donny had a sweetheart, football, and happiness. He was up to his eyeballs in the Program. But we were close, Cube mates, and I hoped some Grace would rub off on me. As it is, Grace did rub off, leaving Donny's name on the 15th Panel West Wall, Line 101. I'm not sure about Grace anymore.

After the fullback, who lived at the Gatehouse tried to take my head out with his cleats over a girl I decided to break a finger on the gym lockers. Anything seemed better than practice. I hated it. Unfortunately, practice continued because I was unsuccessful. I did manage to break my right thumb in a game, but discovered that They would just tape you up—so you could keep playing. Ironically, we won the Hudson Valley conference championship that year and I made the Poughkeepsie News 2nd Team all conference end. Eddie, the black tight end, should have gotten it before me. He was a better football player; but guilty or not, I saved the newspaper clipping anyway.

Greer Leads Grid Stars

Bi-Valley League's Best

Five players from Greer school today were named to the All-star team of the Bi-Valley Football league by the Poughkeepsie New Yorker. Joining them on the roster are three players from Millbrook, two from Red Hook and one from Pawling.

The "dream team" backfield lists Donald Berger and Robert Ildefonso of Greer, John Dondero of Red Hook and Phil Strother, Millbrook's memorable star.

Linemen are ends Robert Moul of Red Hook and Lynn Karn of Millbrook, tackles Robert Russoman of Greer and Kim Tompkins of Pawling, guards

FIRST TEAM		SECOND TEAM
Player, Team	**Pos.**	**Player, Team**
Robert Moul, Red Hook	E	Dan Dewey, Greer
R. Russoman, Greer	T	J. Demboski, Red Hook
John Nicholas, Greer	G	Tony Voight, Greer
Syd Nesbitt, Greer	C	Don. Tangredi, Millbrook
Frank Clouting, Millbrook	G	Jeff Burns, Millbrook
Kim Tompkins, Pawling	T	Fenton Keenan, Greer
Lynn Karn, Millbrook	E	Richard Avella, Red Hook
Donald Berger, Greer	B	Robert Thomas, Red Hook
John Dondero, Red Hook	B	Peter Osis, Greer
Phil Strother, Millbrook	B	William McCord, Pawling
Robert Ildefonso, Greer	B	Dan Fichter, Millbrook

You have to be somebody before you can be nobody. Like the fullback from Gate house was a somebody until 1967 when he became a no-body MIA in Laos.

I was a steady D student in school. Well, there were a few F's. I failed 9th grade too. I was in the embrace of "Mastery learning", a "reductionistic" learning paradigm which presents a collection of ungrounded, disjointed pieces of information in a concerted attempt to have me regurgitate the most miniscule of facts with little understanding required. Chemistry reduced my brain to a puddle. Physics was a presentation of Newton's reassuring clockwork universe. That's right, not the universe we live in. The only learning taking place, however, was in the aerodynamic properties of paper planes and spit ball missiles. English would get me detention too—for "loquaciousness" as the staff liked to put it. Detention was always full and I was there to witness. Detention meant you didn't watch the Friday night movie in the school auditorium. Staff got to watch you.

Mastery learning's end result in teaching "critical thinking" skills according to Bloom's Taxonomy of Education, is a subjective judgment resulting in personal values and opinions with no real right or wrong answers. If I knew better then, I would have been suspicious that the government wanted me firmly planted in the basement of Kohlberg's Socio-moral Judgment Scale. I.E. Have no personal morality other than doing what is "right" to avoid punishment from authorities with superior power. Obedience for it's own sake. Cannon fodder? The government and religious educational paradigm of the day represents the beliefs that we are expected to ultimately think and act on. They present "a world view, 'a way of seeing' which is also a way of not seeing" (Poplin, 1988). Christian soldiers. The perfect graduate—the target of Jesus' parables; the ones who see, but do not perceive, the ones who hear, but do not understand. (Mathew, 13:13.) Bernard Shaw defined those others who give up their will, seeking only to conform to the ideals of the state or church, not for the sake of being themselves, but to be a "good man" as "morally dead and rotten." (Irvine, 1967.) Adam in the Garden had a failure of will, but oddly was created perfect (Gen 1: 31). Go figure.

Never having passed a NYS regents exam in any subject at any time, I was convinced nobody in the State had either. Yet, I got into college. At least to the base of the Ivory Tower. Staff took me to the State campus Spring of my senior year for the entrance examination; bought me a T-bone steak dinner, with baked potato, onions, asparagus and a Molsen Ale. God. A taste of the good life—the outside world. Civilization. I got to drive.

I had asked God for only two things in life so far. The bike, which was since cannibalized and merged with the rest of the bikes on the Farm, and a license to Operate. I got the meal too. God came through and the staff cared about me. Good times. The Farm food sucked, but you'll hear that later.

First semester was financed through working nights at the NY World Telegram & Sun and some HS money. I worked in the photo morgue discovering all sorts of pictures on file. Real life stuff. Accidents, starlets, models, starlets, starlets, starlets . . .

I was an adult, well chronologically anyway. Everything was grand. I was free to eat spam cooked off the steam iron and drink myself silly. Thus, I bombed out of SUNY's Delhi Agricultural and Technical School with the wings of Bacchus firmly attached to my feet. College wasn't for me. The road was. My friend Hank and I found an apartment together about three blocks from his parent's house. That didn't last long.

Living in a 1953 Fix Or Repair Daily (FORD) station wagon from town-to-town, pumping gas, mowing golf courses (for the more productive members of society), washing dishes, cleaning floors and toilets, taught me that proto-box people models were not appreciated. "Not in our town", the police taught me. Some twisted my employer's arm. It didn't take that much to move me. I didn't consider anything "Home". Employers saw me as a lean 1-A draft card. No future. That took 1 1/2 years to learn. Enlistment promised three meals a day, structure, travel and a certificate in idiocy, but the last wasn't on the advertisements.

"Are you afraid of bombs?" asks the Base shrink in Boot Camp.

My first idiotic response, "I don't know, I've never been around one . . . Sir."

I learned to be afraid.

REFS

Ellis, Albert. "Making Ourselves Neurotic." The Humanist, Mar/Apr 1992.

Irvine, William. Bernard Shaw: Selected Plays and Other Writings. New York: Holt, Rinehart and Winston. 1967.

Gibson, Eleanor. "Introductory Essay: What Does Infant Perception Tell Us About Theories of Perception?" J Experimental Psychology, 1987, 13, (4): 515-523.

Minsky, Marvin. "Alienable Rights". Discover, July 1993.

McAuliffe, K. "Get Smart: Controlling Chaos." Omni Magazine (circa 1989).

Poplin, Mary S. "Reductionistic Fallacy in Learning Disabilities: Replicating the past by reducing the present." Journal of Learning Disabilities 1988, 21(7): 389-400.

"Life can only be understood backwards; but it must be lived forwards."—Soren Kierkegaard, "Life"

"CHORES"

Cleaning the dormitory,
Was confusing as Hell.
If you swept early,
The dirt you swept
On the other guy's responsibility,
E.G. The hallway,
Would be back
On your responsibility later,
I. E. The dormitory.
If you swept later,
The other guy
Would know whose dirt
Was on their responsibility,
Because,
My responsibility
Would be clean.

A veritable DILEMMA
In pragmatics.
It never occurred,
To me,
To pick up the dirt
Myself,
Until much later.
I was nine.
Give me a break.

Now I stub
My toe
Kicking the dirt
Under the countertop cabinets,
Because I can't find
The dust pan.

FOOD FOR THOUGHT

I heard the only difference between a fairy tale and a war story was the beginning; the first starts with, "Once upon a time" and the second with, "This is no shit!" So, I'm not sure how this should start being about food, religion, chaos, sweat, and all. It does begin with one of the foods that I remember most, first called by the dining hall staff, "What is this shit?"

Well, plunging in—the (often transient) staff queried the above menu entry always in reference to some kind of roast beast, glistening with what I thought to be a slightly greenish oil-type slick by the time it arrived on my table. Not so. On closer look, the green was the meat—a kind of scaly part and pretty much edges. Aged, I heard for tenderness. (An acceptable practice in those dark commissary days predating tofu and when nitrate was still used for gunpowder.) The ungrateful, of course most of us, cut the way-past-tender meat off the then, edible portion. After Grace.

"Grace", was the shortest homage I ever heard. Before all us kids could pull our chairs out though, staff would get someone else to regurgitate the almost certain (who wants to memorize two homage's?)—"Come Lord Jesus, Be our Guest, Bless us and our food." Predictable, but it rarely worked as the food needed lots more than blessing. Sometimes kids would do, "Good food, Good meat, Good God, let's eat!", but that was usually with substitute staff parents and had little relationship to the food and absolutely no effect on the quality.

We were obviously prayer crazy—insanity at times defined as doing something over and over expecting something different to happen. With a little reason maybe some of us could have replicated the Christian dogma of transubstantiation which holds that once blessed by an ordained priest, a piece of bread becomes in essence the flesh of Jesus Christ. Hello. We wondered if you could do that with liver say and change it to chicken?

Not all the food was green-tinged, maybe an occasional potato, but usually they were powdered potatoes (which are actually loose and wet) and of course the dreaded lima bean. Beets, succotash (lima beans et al) really sucked and my pockets weren't big enough to hold half the food I would involuntarily gag on. And liver—which was supposed to be good for you—not only tasted like nobody anywhere wanted it and that's why we got it so much, but I heard staff say that's where everything goes before it turns to shit. Thank God health wasn't a major concern.

In fairness, they did warn us about the ducks. Freedom fliers brought down, donated and baked, on their way North, with a hail of buckshot. So much, in fact, that the commissary cooks had trouble finding all the shot and probably explained the "donations". All of which underscores a simple truth—"we" are our own "King's Taster", the fellow who checks the King's food for poison or in this case—lead shot. We are smarter, more advanced and can check the staff table first too—to see what they are eating or not eating. Back in the forties and fifties, the Government wasn't as overly concerned about what we consumed orally as it is now and we weren't in a position to sue the orphanage over Buck shot, bacteria or skimpy deserts. I digress.

Peas were green too, but O.K. The most fun peas were slightly soggy and would stick to the ceiling best when launched from your spoon. When "spooning", the pea is placed on the spoon's handle end, which is pointed 180 degrees away from the target. The hand, once cleared by the Forward Staff Observer (yourself usually), strikes the shallow cup end lip downward at 60 degrees, quietly. It's a Newtonian gift. At 90 degrees the pea slams into the ceiling above your head and maybe drops down in your food. Remember, at 60 degrees, with the right force and direction, the pea will clear the ceiling and be in someone else's food way across the dining hall.

Like prayer, the linear destiny of a flying pea was viewed by we concrete thinkers as governed by ordered conditions, no matter how fervently one may have "wished" a pea into a deserving cup. Even with slight initial deviations, there would be no vastly different outcomes. Linear systems are "additive" and serve us well in algebra, the orbit of planets and pea trajectories. They do not serve us well in describing the universe we live in, however, because linear systems can not predict outcomes in non-linear systems such as the brain or the natural world (Barton, 1994). The same can be said about prayer. Actually, forks had the best distance and were quieter, but trust me, you could get hurt on the tines.

The consummate achievement was a pea launched directly into someone's cup without a splash. The pea would settle quickly and upon eventually draining his cup, the stricken kid would always peer through slit eyes to see who was looking and who was not. There were a lot of covert smiles, especially with peas.

Not that there weren't any problems. If the peas were too hard, for example, they would roll off the handle or misfire. Who needed the frustration? Diced carrots stayed well, in a pinch. Corn worked O.K. too, but never stuck like a good pea. Corn was better to eat. Carrots weren't.

I thought there was good food too. I even liked ravioli from a can, but most of the good food was too few and too far between to remember. Except maybe Thanksgiving Dinner. That was always the best. On a daily basis though, toast ranks at the top. I still love toast. The milk was great too—one day from the cow, pasteurized, and so , so cool in the summer. I would drink (steal) a whole quart; snorkeling air while it went down froth and all. Yum. I loved milk as much as the toast. (What's Love? Sid loved the red church wine stored in the vestry, even though it was watered down some. He loved Susie there too. I think the word love gets watered down with all the usage it gets. I know Sid needed to be watered down.)

Thanksgiving Day

Tapioca pudding was supposed to be a desert. Everyone referred to Tapioca as "frog eyes" and separated, screened or tossed the eyes out. Eyes were a misnomer. I thought they were some kind of fish egg. The net result, half-a-pudding. It was more disappointing than a peach-half, which wasn't too bad, just too little.

Pan cake was good. Big flat trays, covered with icing, from the commissary cooks. If you were cool, well-liked, older (bigger), and/or smart you could get a big piece or several. I love cake. And cookies. And doughnuts. And toast.

What's-His-Name? Used to sit on my left at the breakfast table, the best meal excluding Thanksgiving, the freshest, and the one you could consistently identify all the parts. I didn't want to hurt What's-His-Name? but I was real hungry—supper having been something I just pushed around with my fork—thinking, flies wouldn't eat it, yet everyone else is eating supper. How do they do that? (I was thinking too much.)

Well, I was understandably hungry and when I hallucinated that last piece of toast yelling, "Eat me, eat me, eat me"—I grabbed it off the platter with my left hand in front of What's-His-Name? I was hungry. So when he blurts, "That's mine!" grabbing at the now my toast, I stabbed him with my fork. Not enough to really hurt him, I thought, but wouldn't you know it (I wasn't thinking that good)—the damn fork stuck right in the center of his palm. Straight up and quivering. Or his hand was.

Like a tennis match, the rest of us at the table stared at the fork, then What's-His-Name's? quivering lips, then the staff table. Staff were eating obliviously as were all the other kids at the other tables. So we all started to eat, again, after a brief "sweat" while the quivering subsided. Like nothing happened.

I would have remembered the fork kid's name if he had told and so, of course, would everyone else at the institution in which we were housed. Except maybe Mr. Moles who lived in the basement of Daisy Cottage—a three-story stone building with four dormitories on the 2nd floor, surrounding a central bathroom, and two up stair low-ceilinged attic apartments. One, the English teacher with shark's teeth lived in. The other housed, Miss Brunlister, an old spinster type who worked in the

Administration Building doing something—I think maybe in the Sewing Room where the Clothing Coroner who was supposed to provide triage resurrected all the tatters into third or forth-hand clothing darning her magic. That's where the beloved commissary czar and cooks were too. They couldn't have been Russian though as they cursed continually in German.

Miss Brunlister died on the toilet and when we were marched to her Viewing at the chapel—I personally couldn't figure out what was worse; her actual dead body or the visions we all discussed of dying on the toilet with underwear wrapped around your knees. Bizarre stuff, but everyone liked the idea of dying with your boots on. We all were saddened that the commissary crew wasn't lying there instead.

The ur phenomenon that was Miss Brunlister, her essence, was obviously gone, as if time were frozen in the still space surrounding her open coffin. She was toasted. The absence wasn't something you could put your finger on anymore than you could touch a mirage or a molecule. You just knew you were alone in a one-way viewing.

Disquieting? You bet. Even toasters have a life, an existence and if broken, still exude that essence of toaster. Nothing emanated from Miss Brunlister. Not even the hint of a spark. No molecular movement. Dead. I wondered about where her spark went and what we were supposed to be viewing. That wasn't Miss Brunlister lying there. That was what was left of her—the postcard of her journey—stamped and delivered in a wood box. A fancy one at that. Maybe that's what we were supposed to be gawking at.

Well, Mr. Moles was alive and kind of grizzled like the roast beast and also bizarre, but not dead or green-tinged, although there were rumors. Gnarled, yes, but tough in a wizened sense as he rarely left the mysterious basement or had need to we guessed. He never ate in the dinning hall with the other staff. I bet there were some kids who never even knew he lived down there. (They were the ones that never see the Tiger tracks around the water hole.) Most kids avoided him all the time; some, some of the time. That was me. I thought he was some kind of Mystic man. He was the Maintenance man. The force behind the scene. The guy who fixed water pipes, worked on boilers with dials, steam pressure, levers, and valves deep in the bowels of the stone building. He worked in a chaotic system where slight deviations in his initial motions would result in huge differences in outcomes. In actuality, he was an "attractor"—which in physics or math specifies the pattern into which chaotic motions will settle (Van Eenwyk, 1991). But unlike a single-point pendulum attractor, Mr. Moles was a "strange" one in that his particular force never repeated yet always resembled itself. Infinitely recognizable, it was never predictable. Just like life. He was here. He was there. You could never tell whether you would have heat or not and of course, nobody knew what food he ate. There were no wrappers, empty cans, nothing, not a clue. (Eating out was beyond our unworldly comprehension.)

Chaotic behavior occurs in a wide range of physical, chemical and biological systems—most notably, the universe, your brain and boiler systems. Fortunately, in chaotic systems, vast differences settle down or converge into one of four typical patterns commonly termed "strange attractors" (Barton, 1994) and in Mr. Mole's and our Boiler's case—the "attractor" was a simple oscillating cycle of too hot or too cold. He predated Oscar the Grouch, but I think there was a place in his heart for some of us. Especially Donny and me.

Mr. Moles also had a weird looking German micro truck (sic), not bus, truck. A Volkswagen truck like you never saw with all these storage compartments in the side. That's German. (They were the bad guys in WWII, for one, having shot my Uncle's face off with a machine gun.) And he had one of their trucks. I was young and understood good guys and bad guys. Good guys wore white and bad guys shot your Uncle's face off. I didn't understand guns and butter economics, but did know State butter came in 5 Lb blocks, was melted, and brushed onto our toast for expediency. Still impressed, I hung around and learned that bad guys do good work, people get attached to good works, and why Mr. Moles didn't eat free State food in the dinning hall—He said he did once.

He was really pissed off when Donny and I shot nuts, bolts, and stones through his garage wall with our cannon. We made many cannons as the end of the galvanized lead pipes would shred, maybe because we would use too much sulfur. (Who knows? We weren't rocket scientists.) We did know a shredded barrel would destroy its accuracy. We never hurt the truck—just a portion of his garage wall and a window. But we bet he almost had the Big One. Like Miss Brunlister. He wouldn't talk to us for a long while.

The reason we blew up Mr. Moles' garage wall was because, one—it was there, and two—you could see it from the back dormitory where Donny and I lived. Too much temptation. We should have stuck to blowing up cans. Mr. Moles had all the loose pipe collected in and around our dormitory. We had to switch to making grenades out of 2 bolts and a big nut, but they weren't near as exciting.

What's this got to do with food? I don't know, but it's about Mr. Moles who collected all our cannon material and we didn't know what he ate other than it wasn't our fare. We sure put thought into his. Kind of "loose", I know in a psychiatric sense, but bear with me. Our food was the same all over Hope Farm. The Farm being a community of dormitory states. The Gate House, Rap (where Donny and I were sent), Daisy, Apollo, Marcy, Plum, where the little guys still peed in their pants . . . the girl dormitories, all run from the Administration Building.

If you went to the surrounding woods on the boy's side of the Farm, you'd find an old bunker or fort. Over the years kids bonded together and dug bunkers, covering them with anything not tied down, strong enough to hold mounds of dirt. That's where we did bad things like eat stolen bread and government peanut butter. That's where we learned to smoke staff's shortened-to-the-nub cigarette butts—in a bunker. (A real educational environment, but that particular realization was not yet upon us.)

I should tell you about the kid who caught fire hiding his after-dinner cigarette butt up his sleeve. It was really the school building that caught fire though and it's not about food.

Whoa. I was telling you about food, then spoons, forks, Mr. Moles and bunkers like everything is connected or something. Maybe it is, in some kind of chaotic fruitcake existence that everybody makes and few want to eat, but where or what part is Miss Brunlister in? Heaven?

Speaking of. Did you know that bread comes from Heaven through the "sweat" of one's brow? This is abstract and a lot harder than the "eye of the needle" parable, but definitely more food for thought. Such as, Miss Brunlister probably would find it hard to credit the "sweat on my brow" after stabbing What's-his-name for bread.

What does all this mean? Probably nothing as I'm not sure of any absolute truths, but with the linear information I've provided already we can rather accurately compute the temperature of Heaven to see how hot the bread will be, had we earned it the proper way . . . The authority is Isaiah 30:26, "Moreover, the light of the Moon shall be as the light of the Sun and the light of the Sun shall be sevenfold, as the light of seven days." Thus, Heaven receives from the Moon as much radiation as we do from the Sun, and in addition 7x7 (49) times as much as the Earth does from the Sun, or 50 times in all. The light we receive from the Moon is one 1/10,000 of the light we receive from the Sun, so we can ignore that . . . The radiation falling on Heaven will heat it to the point where the heat lost by radiation is just equal to the heat received by radiation, I.E., Heaven loses 50 times as much heat as the Earth by radiation. Using the Stefan-Boltzmann law for radiation, $(H/E) \wedge 4 = 50$, where E is the absolute temperature of the Earth (-300K), gives H as 798K or 525C.

The exact temperature of Hell cannot be computed, however, Revelations 21:8 says, "But the fearful, and unbelieving . . . shall have their part in the lake which burneth with fire and brimstone." A lake of molten brimstone means that its temperature must be at or below the boiling point. That is, 444.6C. (Applied Optics, 11(A14), 1972).

We have then, that Heaven at 525C is hotter than Hell at 445C. I think I'll like Heaven. I love toast hotter than Hell with melted butter and I'm sure lima beans and liver would never make it past St. Peter. (He's a fish guy.) Swordfish steak, sardines, tuna, yes. Pepperoni pizza would only be fair for having lived a good life, strawberry shortcake with whipped cream (I may have to bring myself not having been that good), hopefully Cooney Island hotdogs, the entire peach . . .

REFS

Barton, Scott. "Chaos, Self-Organization, and Psychology." American Psychologist. Jan 1994, 49(1): 5-14.

Van Eenwyk, J.R. "Archetypes: The Strange Attractors of the Psyche". Journal of Analytical Psychology. 1991, 36, 1-25.

"EVERYMAN HAS HIS JEW"

When Arthur Miller wrote,
"Every man has his Jew
And the Jews have their own"
I remembered Larry
Who was a Jew at the Farm.
I called him a "Heeb",
Plenty.
He was smaller than I was.

This hurt Larry who told me so.
I liked Larry forever more
And learned that
Sticks and stones
Will break your bones
And names would make
Larry hurt himself.

B.O. was there too.
Bernie O'name.
He had a concentration tattoo
On his forearm.
So did his brother. What were they doing there?
What was I doing there?

I was a nice seven.
They were Germans
Who shot my Uncle's face off.
I forgot to be Human later
When I killed "Larrys"
For the US Government.
I hope B.O. didn't have to.

"FOOTBALL PRACTICE"

We were playing
Touch football
And Louie
Was "touching"
Way too hard
When I beat the shit
Out of his face
With my USN ring.
The ring was great
As a weapon.
My fists were small
And I was really
Afraid of water
As well as Louie
Who was pissing
Everyone off.
We were never close again
And I didn't join the Navy.
Later Louie managed
To knock up
This Townie,
But didn't feel
Too responsible here
And joined the Marines—
The late '50s
National standard
Of action.
I never did see Louie
In Nam or parenting
And wonder now
If he feels responsible
For anything at all
Yet.

Semper Fi

"INCIDENTALLY"

Have you ever seen someone thrown to the sharks? I don't mean in the movies. I mean real life. We did. At least that's what Lenny's screams sounded like. And who would go through a glass shower door, without a bye-your-leave, straight through—screaming. Blood surely. There had to be sharks in there.

Nobody checked, because we all ran when the glass exploded Lenny and bits onto the bathroom floor in a grand cascade of sound and water. I thought we killed him, but couldn't figure out how. Somebody would pay for this.

There wasn't any sound coming from the bathroom, anymore, because Lenny was quietly picking his barefoot way across the broken glass floor—like walking on hot coals I imagined. His feet are why we threw him in. We didn't worry about his feet. His feet couldn't be killed.

Nobody thought to get a broom. If we could have thought that well—we wouldn't have thrown him in. Anyway, I think it was Lenny's turn to clean the bathroom so it was really unfortunate for him that he messed it up and tough on us that he didn't clean it up fast enough.

When the dorm staff started to nose around . . . I wasn't saying anything at first, but "I did hear it" and nobody else was saying anything either because of the code between us. Great idea leaving it to Lenny anyway, after all, why did he go through the glass door?

Lenny was not creative. So maybe it was a bad idea leaving it to him. He said we forced him in while the water was running. Can you imagine our indignation? Us? Touch Lenny. "Preposterous" (In so many words) we told staff. Touch a guy with hardened dirt for fingernails—the guy whose socks stood up by themselves, whose very aroma gave new meaning to "stink". The guy was a slob. He never saw a shower until we introduced him and he couldn't tell the difference between a glass door and a shower curtain. That was obvious. He didn't even know how to turn off the water. He wasn't dull though—he knew panic. And he would get to know what a snitch was.

I said there wasn't a ten-foot pole I would touch him with. (You have to try when you are young.) My dorm mates agreed. Someone said twelve feet. Maybe it was the other dorm kids? The door stuck? It was new. He could have slipped! But no, Lenny fingered us.

So what could THEY do to all of us? Fine us? Lock us up? There wasn't anyplace to go anyway, so THEY fined us. In this case, THEY was The Administration Building this time, although THEY was the often transient dorm staff. (There were four dorms in our building—that would be 40 of NY City's finest to manage. Go figure.) Don't ask who was in The Administration Building. That's another story and this is about sharks, I think.

We earned 15 cents (.15) an hour (x). The door cost $60. There were ten (10) of us in our dorm, only five of us pushed him in, leaving 4 innocents, but whose counting? THEY are. So:

$$(10)15(x) = \$60;$$

$$x = 40 \text{ hours apiece}$$

Not bad, at that rate we could have thrown Lenny to the "sharks" every few months and, incidentally, now you know Algebra. (We will all become rocket scientists and/or space cadets because of our flaws.) In due time, I also received detention for "loquaciousness" talking about "poles". We had to look the word up. More incidental learning.

Detention was on Fridays when everyone got to watch the Friday movie in the school auditorium and the staff got to watch you. Actually, I learned enough in study hall every night and detention Fridays to get through high school "incidentally" probably because my school book was open wide enough to ooze out learning, while shielding my sleeping head—which characteristically drooled on my hand, on top of the table, cushioning my cheek, as learning slowly penetrated my skull, hidden from the staff. I did like to read when I wasn't drooling, but then, maybe because I drooled on my hand—I had those shark dreams, where everyone is floating around their torpedoed merchant ship in one dense mass, their legs treading. I never wanted to join the Navy after those dreams. My destiny had changed, just from drool.

The beautiful part about the new glass door—it closed, but as you know, to no avail. Lenny sure didn't learn anything. He wasn't in the shower long enough and "popped" out of the shower almost as fast as we got him in—like some kind of gross balloon. We had to come up with $60 and his socks began to walk. Not literally, but someone said they moved.

Well, bottom line, if cleanliness has anything to do with godliness—I'm not sure who's going to Heaven last—Lenny or his socks, because Heaven works in mysterious ways. You have to love incidental learning though, that's no mystery. (Press a swollen balloon between your hand and table. What happened?)

We got $30 from Lenny, we "Land Sharks."

"XMAS PLAYS REVISITED"

In our senior year,
Tony played Joseph
In the Xmas play.
The play was the same
Every year.
I didn't learn shit.
I was the "light man".
The guy who dimmed
The lights
In the Xmas play.
I went to Nam
A few years later
And dimmed
Vietnamese lights.
I had the same shitty feeling,
Only worse,
But I was participating.
God was trying
To tell me something.
What?

"INSTANT SUCCESS
OR TOTAL FAILURE"

J.F.K. said, "Ask not what your Country can do for you, but what you can do for your country." That quaint syntax was great for sedating your reason asleep. What he really said was, "Ask not what your Flag can do for your (maybe) everlasting spirit, but what you can do for the Flag." Translated into politics of the day, "Kill the yellow Canaanites over the hill, for they are killing themselves." Cardinal Spellman of NYC agreed, but I think it was because the Vietnamese were red.

The Flag wanted to clean up Vietnam's home. Great, they all had dirt floors, this could go on forever. The Pentagon factory workers cheered, politicians shifted shiftily, mothers wailed, and later kids looked at their number. Some dazed. POTUS Johnson eventually clarified the objective, exhorting the troops at Cam Ranh Bay to "come home with that coonskin on the wall." (Newsweek, 1966).

Two years prior, the Boot Camp psychiatrist finally cut to the chase, asking me, "Are you afraid of bombs?" and I responded, "I don't know, I've never been around one . . . Sir" which propelled me toward the 3441st Bomb School and a "sensitive" position amongst the only military personnel at risk of dismemberment or death on a daily basis—the USAF Munitions Specialists. We were eventually paid extra Hazardous Duty pay and given the motto, "Stay alive so that others may die". With more training and time, some of us became attached to EOD (Explosive Ordnance Disposal) and the motto morphed to "Instant success or total failure".

Dark. The landing field lights were pinpoints, the C-130 transport a camouflaged outline; its big cargo door opened like a giant mouth and swallowed us up in the silence of gear clinking and duffel bags. The orders-of-the-day, "Get your head between your knees when the landing alarm clangs." No tourist glide, we came in like a plunging elevator; bell clanging, dim red, no lights, the crew not wanting to get shot on approach. Kind of like the "controlled" crash landings cargo pilots practice when there's not much aboard. I was impressed. The aircrew were serious, something I had trouble with. The only serious trait I would admit to was in keeping all my limbs. That's why I rode in the rear—so the C-130 landing struts wouldn't impale me on impact. That was real. And so, apparently, was Vietnam.

The bomb dump perimeter was some barbwire; two swivel 50 calibers manned by South Vietnamese ARVN (whose reputation to not "take a bullet" preceded them), and a bunker that needed far more sandbags. A broad pimple the far side of the base camp. No igloos to contain explosions. Inside the perimeter—the Big Bang, Little Nagasaki.

Dropping our first bombs in the Iron Triangle, we flattened the huts to rubble and debris. More bombs blew the rubble and debris to dust and ashes, and after that we dropped Napalm burning the dust and ashes to nothing. Then the village that was not a village anymore was now our village. Sometimes we hit other targets. We hit a Buddhist Pagoda 3 times by "accident", a Catholic church once (really by accident), and the Cao Dai temple twice again "accidently" to name a few of the consequences over 3,500 sorties we of the 307th TFS Munitions provided for.

Sorties in other provinces are reported to leave a woman with both arms burned off by our Napalm and her lids so badly burned she couldn't close her eyes. When it was time to sleep, her family put a blanket over her and two of her children were killed by the air strike that maimed her (1). The outskirts of Quangngai was soon pounded—the body count claiming 500 VC (Vietcong) KBA (killed by air). After the attack, three out of four seeking treatment for "jellied gasoline" burns at the Vietnamese hospital were village women who told a different, but familiar story (2).

Over fifteen hundred villages in South Vietnam were destroyed by '65's end to deny the VC food and shelter, a few by Zippo, most by Dow's Napalm. Villages suspected of harboring VC were subjected to "search and destroy" rules of action; killing all men of military age, the women, children and old men herded to refugee camps, their homes razed, and their villages burned. Large areas were declared "free fire zones" and anyone within them—including children—were considered the enemy. Villages outside the free fire zones met different fates although it was the same war dance. My Lai was one. Colonel Oran Henderson, charged with covering up the My Lai killings stated, "Every unit of Brigade size has its My Lai hidden someplace" (3).

Nobody knows what happened, everyone has a theory. An A-1 pilot hit his starter switch firing the black powder starter cartridge which in turn causes a small starter turbine to spin (sometimes out of) the starter housing like a buzz saw into the fuse of a 500 lb. GP fragmentation bomb. An inboard explosion on one of the 3rd Bomb Wing's Canberra's. A chemical-delay fuse was inadvertently armed. A cluster bomblet detonated. A sapper got through the wire. Mortar.

The Army's 173rd from Vung Tau Province had to police the body part remains from what was left of the 3rd Bomb Wing's Munitions Specialists. The Grunts are supposed to get used to body parts (frequenting land mines et al). We in ordnance aren't, but do keep a dog tag on our boot so they can match our halves up OK. We laugh a lot and trade empty 20mm ammo cans for C-Rats to help the grunts off the mud and we get more food after we tell them they can heat their food with a pinch of the Comp C they're issued. The caveat being, "Don't try to stomp it out."

South Vietnamese humped munitions with us. Human forklifts. My favorite, sandaled, open shirt so far removed from stay press, with his sleeves rolled up, and bowed legs humped enough munitions to blow half his country away. He worked hard. Since our Vietnamese friends were known to pace off, sometimes marking coordinates during the day to aid in mortar and rocket attacks, I would sometimes look into his eyes and wonder if he too were a VC or Viet Minh (the older guys who fought the French). Everyone looked the same, but he did look different than the intense black eyes impaled on stressed Buddha's in the POW compound. His eyes appeared always moist, as if he were continually weeping or oozing his sadness. I'll not forget the ones in the compound either. They burned hatred. I wished there was another way to the Bomb Dump, but there wasn't. Now I can't remember the path at all.

Live ordnance almost never came back being dropped on anything black and moving. E.G. Peasants and water buffaloes. There was an obvious reason for this. So when a USN fighter bomber was refused carrier landing at sea, because his A-4 Skyhawk had a hung bomb which defied repeated attempts to release or jettison, he was redirected to we on the ground at the

Bien Hoa AB. The hung bomb didn't drop from his touchdown jolt, so we got word to bring a bomb hoist lift down to the arming pads to retrieve this miscreant munition. Well, miscreant may be a bit harsh. Bombs pretty much do what they are supposed to, it's the fuzes that don't. A possibility here, since the Skyhawk was carrier based, salt spray could have affected the arming units, release units or electrical assemblies negatively. This Skyhawk also had ejector type bomb racks, not free-fall ones. Ejector bomb racks serve the same purpose as free-fall racks, but differ in that they use electrically fired impulse cartridges to push the bomb free of the bomb rack as "fast movers" create a vacuum that will hold the bomb under the wing after a free-fall release.

The impulse cartridge hadn't fired, the in-flight lock hadn't released or the fault was in the pylon assembly itself. Wrong or whatever. The immediate problem turned out to be that the hung-up 500 pound GP HE MK 82 bomb was found to be fuzed with a chemical long-delay and equipped with an anti-withdrawal device instead of the typical M904/905 with two delay settings and an observation window to display the possible fuze conditions. The anti-disturbance device would cause the bomb to detonate if that fuze were removed in the normal fashion—that is by simply unscrewing it from the rear well of the bomb, because a little kidney bean shape situated in the bomb well thread would slip into a hole in the fuze threads and . . . so it would have to be frozen with CO_2 or immobilized with quick-set plaster and then unscrewed.

As the aircraft had been catapult-launched from an aircraft carrier, flown an attack mission, and made a rough emergency landing . . . the chemical nose fuse was considered to be possibly armed as well. I.E. Having suffered many physical shocks and time in flight, the chemical could have eaten its way through the safety features in the fuze by now and the firing pin could be released with more disturbance or time. No place to hang around. (The first EOD death recorded was A2C Sanderson training on a chemical-delay fuze. And, of course, Sergeants Hubbard, Pollard, Fidiam, and Capt McFeron were all killed safing bombs, some with chemical-delays, as they were clearing the cooked and strewn bombs left over from the massive May16th's morning explosions.)

There are SOPs. Plan A in this case to hold the chemical nose fuze upright and immobile while it gets unscrewed after taking off the bomb lugs and spinning the bomb anti-clockwise as it rests on top of the MJ-1 bomb lift cradle. But this bomb had its initial problem—it was still hung up on its rack on the wing of the Skyhawk and wouldn't come off. It couldn't be spun.

Plan B removes the whole bomb, fuzes, and rack from the wing of the aircraft, delicately putting the entire assembly onto our truck, and moving it to a ravine at the far end of the runway where it could be safely detonated using a Comp C plastic demolition charge. At least, that was what was voted on to happen.

There wasn't enough time for creative genius much less Plan B, because there wasn't enough time. The Skyhawk pilot, still alive, was almost into Base Ops when he went back to his plane to get his forgotten maps. Bad timing. He was standing on the wing, SUDDENLY disappearing in a silent cloudburst, as we approached from the Bomb dump. Good timing. A light year moment later, the shock wave announced the arming pad going up in a black bellowing eruption of cooking ammo, burning Jet-A fuel, and at least one pilot who wasn't living on borrowed time anymore staining the clear blue sky. Stunned, we caught our breath as intermittent pebbles finally pinged off the hood of our bomb hoist truck, and dust settled over us. We exhaled and breathed in some of his DNA. The 173rd eventually found his name tag, but it took three days to figure out he was a USAF major on an exchange tour with the USN. It's hard to identify a pink mist. He was gone, except for the memory of him—standing on a wing, clutching paper . . .

Total failure.

Tomorrow will be the first or last day in the rest of our lives.

REFS

(1) Langguth, Jack. NY Times Jun 5, 1965.

(2) Charles Mohr Times of Saigon. Sep 6,1965.

(3) Zinn, Howard. Postwar America 1945-1971. Cambridge, MA: South End Press. 2002

"SEPARATED WITH HONOR"

Have you ever heard the Jewish expression, "Don't piss on my head and tell me it's raining outside"? Neither had I when the government was pissing all over us without even mentioning the whole Pissant Program was raining too. A lot of us suspected though.

Leaving El Uotia, North Africa, that part of unbroken sand and silence but for the craters, strafing, and occasional bomb run for civilization created an uneasy ambivalence. Civilization sucked. This was ending my second isolated tour, because nobody in the 401st had been here previously, I was qualified for remote duty, and the El Uotia Bomb & Gunnery Range was the furthest I could get from Uncle Sam, Mickey Mouse, people, noise or thinking at the time . . . or maybe it was because I forgot about 10 minutes after hearing the order to teach a class I was scheduled for at Torrejón AFB . . . you know—a "Siberian" assignment.

El Uotia Tower

Calling me back to Torrejón for separation and then America reminded me of my Grandfather passing through Ellis Island in NYC after being inoculated with US bureaucratic babble. He and Kafka would have appreciated the absurdity here in Spain, but I was too numb from a "ding" in my consciousness or maybe like my "spirit" was totaled . . . I don't know—I'm not Freud. I wasn't appreciating anything. Anyway, on the exterior, the old model 12672818 was shuffling, but un-dented. The luster was gone from the eyes, at least on the inside. ETOH still propelled the body.

A clerk asked, "How would you like to go back to America? By Boat or plane?"

Withdrawn and all, there was no hesitation now in leaving Uncle Sam and his friend Mickey. Neither one of them was responsible either. I feared flying now too, at least more than water, so I said, "Boat." I'd leave earlier. What a fox.

"You can't", the clerk says.

"Huh?" I inarticulate, "Why did you ask then?"

"Because it's on the form", he says without blinking.

Absurd? Not really Franz. This kind of shit is normal. Why else would anyone choose to live in a desert? "Normal" in The World is a chosen standard of irrational behavior. It's also normal to die. I think I'm starting to think too much.

The plane didn't crash as it landed at McGuire AFB. This was not "good news" to anyone, but me. Civilization. Well, the Transient Base Barrack. I was a still shadow. Another shade blending into the rows of barren beds. A civilized dormitory desert that lacked the warm tones of the sand and heat of the sun. God wasn't here. I was lonely.

In the desert you could count on the serenity. Here, I felt a disaster was imminent. A buffer would be nice. I thus spent two weeks back pay on ETOH. Four years of savings.

Adjustment? I waited over the weekend so some 2nd Lt. would honor my paper with his graduated ink. I didn't know about the Peter Principle, but knew I had risen to my level of incompetency—I was worthless to the military. The Lt. was just starting out and would be promoted until his hand could no longer sign his signature. Then he would be stuck at that level and assigned a sergeant with a rubber signature stamp.

Entry into the workforce? Sure, I was given a card that in myopic print reads, "civilian occupation code 6-54.093 Explosives Operator". Go forth and be productive. (The last is my humor.) Four years of pressure. Separated one day early. Quite decent of them, don't you think?

I didn't know what to do with my life. Life appeared to suck in a significant degree. I lasted one week with UPS and three at Beneficial Finance before I thought of school.

School. ETOH. Drugs. Sex. I even got that ass-backwards. This type Regime though appeared more appealing than pumping gas for the more "productive" members of society or making bombs at Red Stone Arsenal to destroy little brown people with flatter noses than us. So it was off to NY State for me. Resident tuition. Just like my friend "Pineapple" did. I wished I were him. Dull, but not dead.

I remember arriving at the train station thinking I had told Mother I was coming. Maybe I didn't. I couldn't remember. So I sat on my duffle bag for hours remembering I didn't have any money wondering why I thought I had called. I'd still be there or eventually arrested for vagrancy, which ever came first, if a taxi driver hadn't given me 10 cents to make a call. I was honored. I guess. Maybe the uniform was. Whatever. He didn't know that I actually was one of them "baby burner" participants. I could have told him how to make explosives out of his own urine or I could have told him what a monk's skull does when it gets immolated, but he wasn't thinking about any of that. How could he? That was my World. This place was another Planet, another World, another life. It didn't feel real at all. He didn't seem real. What in the Hell was I going to do? (I eventually wound up sitting on my duffle bag at a dirt crossroad 20 miles North of Haifa, Israel willing to go in any direction the next vehicle came 4 yrs later, but that's another story.)

Two days later my Mother and Stepfather's capitalist friends arrived for a tie and jacket affair at his home in the East coast Beverly Hills (Scarsdale). They wanted to know about Vietnam and called me forth from washing their dishes I had entered a trance with to regale them with the on-going destruction of the communists they feared so much as I stood atop a plush Persian rug in Stepfather's study wondering if my Mother even knew my birthday or what to say to Elites who couldn't tell the difference between a "piss tube" and a latrine. I settled for the short form and would have married the rug.

"We burn the Vietnamese alive, melt their limbs off, destroy hundreds of their villages, murder and maim thousands of innocent men, women and children with bomb fragments, personnel mines, rockets, and cannon fire. We mine their rice paddies, litter their trails with cluster bomblets, and destroy their forests with toxic chemicals and incendiaries. We relocate them to ghettos surrounded by wire so they can't support the VC and conduct the most indiscriminate and massive program for the political murder of "suspected collaborators" since the Nazi death camps (i.e. Phoenix). They hate our guts. Many are starving between us destroying their food before the VC can steal it and the VC stealing it before we can destroy it. They would eat fish heads if they had too. I didn't mention the chemical-delay and anti-disturbance fuzing or the POW eyes impaled behind barbed wire—hatred indelibly printed on mine forever.

They would not accept or could imagine my truths. Their comforts so great, their beliefs so crystallized. They wanted a Guide Book Tour.

"Nobody eats fish heads!" they squealed.

"THE TRUTH TO THE MATTER"

Truth cannot be found in abstract theory, but only in existence.
Kierkegaard

Frank had a lopsided smile stamped in the middle of an aftershave. Like the Mona Lisa, his alert black eyes suggested an awareness of reality much deeper than his plump capitalist friend. We liked each other from the start.

We met in Harlem bar. His boss liked to buy, which was great since I had just quit collecting for a finance company. A job I was recommended as it was a "white collar" and therefore, respectable one. Where for ten dollars, crushed people with crumpled Washington's could defer their twenty-dollar payment one more month. If they were unfortunate enough to own a TV or car, these were fair game for the company as well. I could let the Loan Company rot.

I was looking for a dollar with more conscience and the capitalist destroyed trees and insects through Frank. How karmic. As my adjustment to civilization, the Government provided my separation papers with a related civilian occupation 6-54-098 Explosives Operator. I was hired immediately. I took his manicured hand and pumped the rings up and down. Frank gave me a wry smile. We were going to have a blast.

Frank was paratrooper in Vietnam. I have a fear of heights and flying (among other things). We worked well together. He never seemed to get excited, but that wry smile came with the truth that only bird shit and idiots fall from the sky. Anyway, he accepted my fears and idiocy. I fell three times altogether that first year—and he still worked with me. Even after he refused to the time I got knocked out on a Long Island job.

We drank a lot, but he didn't do drugs. "Too paranoid", he'd say. I loved it. Being nailed to the couch, unable to will my feet to move. (I really could have, but there wasn't much point in leaving Mello land.) It was nice to stay focused on one or two things—music or nothing. But even "nothing" was full of thoughts. Staying focused was important. Frank enjoyed the atmosphere, popping beer one-after-the-other. He wasn't too happy though. He was depressed.

I could understand. A beer can, Frank and I were different but not by much. The can has content—we were more aware, but went flat just as fast. We had a head before the Government sucked it off. We could have foamed with the best of the other "canscripts", but we were flatheads after Vietnam. Too many suds spilled over, following the SALT (Selected Alternative Lethal Traumas). We didn't sit around going flat. We were splashed on paper, splashed in a Dump, in LZs, Government inspected, 4.5% aware. Dumb as a can. A little more aware.

We didn't talk about school. I was trying to find truth and happiness in Aristotle's Poetics, tea leaves and the I Ching. Frank knew it was all frog pebbles, except Hamlet's PTSD, but was decent enough not to challenge my aim. He liked Shakespeare's—kill all the lawyers first. Right to heart of the justice matter. But, if it was the "nitty-gritty", he'd let the lawyers take his underwear. He was burnt out. That's why his eyes were so intensely black. Burnished cinder. His wry smile a paradoxical testimony to the Stoic way.

Frank's truth came from his experience. That's why I liked him. He was not normal. Who knows how many ponchos he vibrated back with under the rocka-rocka-rocka-rocka chopper blades. There seemed to be a lot, especially when they were all lined up in a row, shoulder to shoulder, waiting for their last flight home. We never talked about what we did. The understanding that we shared a common truth was enough. We knew what people were capable of.

We also knew: that having your body parts at the end of the day beat the alternative; loud, sudden noises in a helicopter will get your undivided attention, there is no Jesus nut, "chicken plates" were not something ordered in a restaurant, a free fire zone had nothing to do with economics, PETN cord can make a dull day fun, the SHIT equation can be used to measure pucker power (I.E. S[suction]+H[height above ground]+I[interest in staying alive]+T[amount of tracers coming your way]), and lastly thousands of Vietnam veterans earned medals for bravery every day. A few were even awarded.

We didn't know about the government's studies on the cancer causing properties of Agent Orange (AO). The government was into denying everything. We didn't know there were hundreds of live American prisoners in Indochina and for "political reasons" their existence was officially denied. We didn't know everybody was expendable and how quick the policy people were to "abandon" anybody, who might be seen as a political liability, to a "toxic waste dump". I.E. the POW/MIA Office (Peck, 1991).

We also knew that Frank's wife left him nothing but the lawyer's mail. Mental cruelty. A severe blow to the social order. The only person Frank tortured was himself, with his own yardstick. How would you measure your life? Against an elephants? A Spring flower? Is it "up", "down", the "pits"? Great? Less than satisfactory? Achy? Bubbly? Numb?

I was numb for a long time trying to get out from all of it. What a horror show. Happiness in the context of pain. Survival. Why?

If you were to measure your life, whose yardstick would you use? Yours? Where did you get it? Whose ruler? Yours?

We Americans measure the World by inches and feet—a standard passed to us from some ancient king who had a part-of-his-thumb called an inch. Terrific! We agreed on something. It was a start. Do you want to measure your life with someone else's "thumb"? I wouldn't trust someone else's thumb to excavate my outhouse.

Your existence as a human being—is that part of the stick under your nose. Not that part of the stick concerned with disciplines or role models—in which even circus fleas or apes could measure themselves. Trust me, we are different.

You existence as a Human Being (verb) is that part of the stick covered with Mores, Regulations, Peer Pressures, Theology, and everyone else's truth but yours. Cultural paint on top of your uniqueness.

What is it to be Human? Do we use a Druid stick, Aztec, Hindu, Christian, Technocrat, Bureaucrat, Administer, Hamburger Flipper, Student Drop-Out, or Yuppie stick? Obsessive-Compulsive sticks? Hysterical? Shit, we continually club ourselves with someone else's yardstick.

Use your own. Not Hitler's, Fallwell's, not Kennedy's, not your Mom's. Your own. Can't find it? Get paint remover. It's there. Underneath a lot of Other's paint, colored Ontologic truth.

I didn't help Frank. I was too busy relieving aches with diversion and escaped into literature ala drugs. The Veterans Hospital? Theory. "You should be adjusted, therefore you are sick." "You have a personality disturbance. A problem with authority. An Adjustment Disorder." "Don't take your drugs, take ours." Frank wouldn't touch drugs—until They pushed them down his throat.

The VA? An agent of the Program, not life. In truth, people begin healthy, the Program is sick; peopled by lemmings in a submarine under the Ocean of Existence. I know. I worked two years on a VA acute psychiatric ward.

At school, kids were just as confused. Jumping up and down in petroli oil, hashish, mescaline, THC, acid, peyote, and cocaine. They were in the womb of their parent's tuition money. Not everyone. There wouldn't have been enough for those of us who really wanted it. (Today Veteran Affairs allows VA physicians to prescribe medical marijuana for PTSD [http://www.nytimes.com/2010/07/24/healt . . . wanted=all] while the Federal and State governments lock up veterans in States where it's illegal. Go figure. I have two felony arrests self-medicating my service-connected Anxiety Disorder.)

Kent State blew them away. They had no idea what man or the Government is really capable of. If they knew, the students would have had to hold their own draft to find demonstrators. I would have been no. 32 on the Government draft. Karma. I couldn't relate to my classmates, potential draft dodgers all. They were avoiding life too, only differently.

Frank crashed his bike and what hair he had stayed messed up. He looked like shit. I felt like shit. I'd been married for a couple of months. It should have been annulled before the cake got stale. She escaped her mother (long after her father did) for a name and bed. I knew this, but couldn't hurt her except through crimes of omission. Mental cruelty. I couldn't shake my world for hers. She found someone else. I let her have all the junk. Frank didn't expect anything from me.

We left for Canada shortly after his crash. R&R. I wanted to hear grass grow. I hated the City, hated the noise, the social bullshit, the money, and alienation. Now that I had thought about it, survival wasn't as important as the question—Why?

What is it to be Human in this morass of fluorocarbons, nukes, disease, corporations, lawyers, politicians, capitalists, greed, cash registers, consumerism, relaters, money lenders, stock market bulls, leftists, rightists, conservatives, radicals, rapists, sadists, liberals, psychiatrists, "educators", directors, lawyers (get them first), life insurance salesmen, dictators, sheep (scratch that, they're animals), perverts, degenerates, slime, poisonous snakes, snakes, spiders (I've heard they're animals theory), tax, pollution, litter, crime, tall buildings, cigarettes, money, advertisements, TV writers, and bras?

Sex is O.K. Hamburgers are ruinous.

Who the Hell is responsible for this shit? I used to think that there was possibly a Department of Irreducible Responsibility Transfer (DIRT). DIRT would be a necessary function in American bureaucracy, the American way of life. Without DIRT we would be buried in responsibility—guilt. DIRT buries guilt and if all the contemporary vaults are occupied, shoots responsibility into an orbit around "economy" or the "flag"—quite distant from the orbit of conscious gravity you know.

DIRT is not a member of the cabinet or corporate board. Actually it is an obscure department with high-tech spin communications, located in the bowels of administration, staffed completely with lawyers—a revered form of bacteria. Think of it. Eight hundred Forty Thousand plus in this country alone. This litigious society can orbit anything to a place of no accountability. Crowding is not the problem in orbit that shredding machines have become here behind Earth's closed doors.

The "buck" stops here proclaim numerous bronze plaques affixed to corporate desks, political tongues, and industrial chimneys. Of course they mean the dollar "buck", not those conscious ones. "The portion of wealth held by the top 1% in the U.S. has exploded from 22% in 1979 to about 42% today (Congressman Obey, 1996). Yep, the "buck" is stopping way up there. Today we far surpass Great Britain's past class-based society of castles and peerages in income disparity. Why? Congressman Obey stated that much of this economically disastrous, morally deficient disparity is driven by public policy formed by the "very economic elite that most benefited from them." You know—the calculating men who support "work for welfare mothers" and "welfare subsidies for corporations".

Sometimes the dollar "buck" bottlenecks at the desk of the more productive members of our society—dribbling over in a "trickle" down to me. I have to pass it on in a well-worn "hand-to-mouth" existence, but I'm not passing my responsibility. I'm all for a responsible anarchy now.

Frank sat in silence, he'd heard it all before. His black eyes, half-hooded, never wavered from the passenger window. I felt like John Voight in Midnight Cowboy. I was there with Frank. Which was good. He perked up somewhere in Quebec, rowed the distance to a campsite and laughed when we burned our new tent. Actually, it melted. The wonders of modern petroleum science. Frank took the boat a lot to fish somewhere other than the camp. I kept the rifle.

When we returned to civilization, Frank shot himself in the back of head. So much for laughter. It wasn't a gesture. Frank couldn't face anything. He hurt.

I caught up with Frank locked in the State mental hospital. (No, not the VA.) He had that wry smile again, like he crashed his suicide. The abashed boy in him, sneaking a signal past the dead adult. The only way he could get out of the hospital was to say that he wouldn't kill himself. That took awhile. He was trapped and lying didn't occur to him or he wouldn't.

Drugged, zapped, and sandwiched between manics, schizophrenics, sociopaths, and the new, fast-filling group of Borderline personalities. Frank wasn't crazy. He was alienated. Frank wasn't disoriented. He was in pain and didn't know where the brass ring was. Neither did I. The staff wanted him to believe their truths about life, but he wouldn't disbelieve his own.

When Frank got out, I was out of school. No longer did he look like shit. He was well groomed, clean shaven and angry about being locked up, part of the Program. His eyes had a fierceness to them when he asked for money to get to Argentina. He borrowed it. He left.

I hope he found a new truth for himself. Or just another yardstick.

"BIG QUESTION"

Do we transcend Nature,
The animal world,
Through our own awareness?
Or do we live
In a world of stimulus-response?
Both?
Just action?
Do we think too?
Is the quality of our thought
Different than a sponge?
A giraffe?
Does this make us different
Than the animals?

If so,
Then perhaps we are more
Than "social animals"
Maybe we are Human,
True, an animal
But different
We are responsible
For our actions.

Or are we?

Maybe politicians are.

God doesn't want to be.

"HUMANS"

Lemmings are in lockstep. Rigid, but at least they are not manning a submarine under the "Ocean of Existence". What is Existence? but the Worlds of Nature, Mind, and Human relationships. Pain/pleasure, life/death, the growth of awareness. Yes, Existence embraces the duality of Nature.

Does one experience this duality in the bowels of urban existence, in society? Sure, there's misery, suffering, degradation, greed, cash registers, HAPPY consumerism, and the awareness that this is indeed a sick "Program". A Program which assumes each citizen's responsibility and answers to no one; answers to no god either. What better way to avoid responsibility than to give it to a corporation or politician? They give it to some teleological truth and thus, responsibility is far, very far removed from Humans.

What's good for the masses is good for the individual. What Bullshit. I am a representative mass living amidst a wasteland of responsibility. We have more mechanisms to move responsibility than we do dirt. We are in a horror scene of alienation and mercantilism. "An honest days work" meant that you didn't make much when I was a kid. Who's responsible for this mess? Everybody is a hamburger flipper.

All man-made. Self-made victims in an implied delusion of survival and security . Does retirement insure you of experiencing life? Does insurance protect you from pain? It's a pain-in-the-ass to pay for it. Why do you think Humans need insurance? Because they can't trust their fellow man to be responsible for his/her actions?

We put non-responsible people in institutions.

"SHE AND I MET LAST NIGHT"

In a nervous energy
Unrehearsed.
She came alone trailing breadcrumbs
Made of nothing except loneliness,
From city fuming smog
To watch the Blue Ridge season
Turn toward winter aging yellows and reds,
In leafy sunsets
Amidst the White Pine,
Cloud glossed green,
Three thousand feet above the Mainstream.
A hint of loss
Shadowed her almond eyes,
Clinging to soft-turned lips,
Whispering unspoken witness
To a broken heart.
Yet.
Her rainbow mind,
Undaunted,
Her eyes sparkled as sky diamonds
And the moments were full
Of seeds like a dandelion collision
Our paths met,
Under a crystal Milky Way,
When night gathered
The color of Midnight
And swallowed me.

Time turned to dream
As we laughed
And my heart
Did gyre and gimble
Drinking her pleasure,
Endlessly,
We touched, sizzling,
Mad and moonly struck,
And the moments were traced
By hungry fingers
Into memory.

"SHE WAS AN AMERICAN DREAM"

And he saw her first
At 11 Watts Street,
Under a red NYC neon light,
In the So Ho District,
Waiting to be bought.
She wasn't exactly
Brand new but,
She was well built,
And all decked out
With new treads
And a leather skirt,
Back rested,
And ready to dance
For the right price.
Purring promisingly,
Just stroking the right button;
He had to have her,
There was no reverse,
Money was no object,
And being fortunate,
With manly gifts,
Was soon on top of her
Trying her out.
She squealed
At first,
He being really rusty,
But soon shifted
Her over more comfortably
And smoothed
Into rhythmic pounding

Fluids pumping,
Heads knocking,
Cleaning her pipes
A mile-a-minute,
She wasn't even panting,
Almost losing himself
Pushing hard her
Bulbous body,
In ecstasy,
She was screaming,
Until braking,
She shuddered
To a stop,
Trembling.
God,
She was the sweetest
Motorcycle
He'd ever had.

For more information contact:
American Dream Machine
11 Watts St
New York, NY 10013
(212) 343-2601

(Apologies to: ee cummings)

"CHOCOLATE HEAVEN"

She came early in the night,
Some timid taps
Birdly soft
On my door,
Breathless was her beauty,
And the door was dumb
As I was mute
But not the dog—Spencer,
"Bark Bark Bark, Bark Bark Bark Bark"
("Someone has come, to kill us all")

And I heard her voice
To me alone
Carried on perfumed words
Tasting like chocolate
To my mind,
"Hi there Dan"
And dazed,
I went
To Heaven.

"DRACO CONSTIPATUS"

Once my six year old, Amity, asked, "Dad, why does the Sun stay still when we go to town?" She looked for meaning as the Celestial music showered illusion on our carbon dust.

The grass froze as the wind paused breathless on the ridge, suspended. "Truth" was near, babbling the long dull tale of Butterfly Effects and tangible phenomena across the invisible floor of my dragon-dad cave. Shit.

The paltry facts to blue skies, star twinkle and a Copernican sun were ill trade for wonderment. So when she asked, I remembered Einstein's graffiti. I.E. "Science would describe music as a series of air wave fluctuations." Really. If Science were a vehicle, wonderment would be a road kill. Better that she read the notes later for her own answers to the Score and it's Composer.

Her bright eyes were fixed in calm wonderment. Waiting. A young medicine woman, unafraid as she faced heavy scales cold as the memory of Death Days.

'All is complex illusion generated from simple initial conditions subjected to iterative deterministic randomness between dust-to-dust sometimes known as Chaos—the sheep in wolves clothes' (Pool, 1989). Or simpler yet—poof to the accompaniment of music, whispered silently Dragon's string of depressed truth beyond the Veil of Relativity at his cave entrance.

She was too young to slay a dragon dad's truth no matter how dressed. Just a glimpse and her pants would darken from angst. She was dry as she was innocent. I wished I were her. Well, a medicine man, not a dragon. Testosterones are hell, but I'll keep them. Scales suck.

I, the Dragon, equivocated, suggesting a vastly different truth outcome with just a slight change in her initial condition, "Actually, my daughter, the sun is not where you see it."

'Wonder about that', I thought, as the wind resumed lyric background to the music of the spheres.

Nirvana . . . erodes through living and inklings.

"Dad, I have to go to the bathroom."

So did I, but for a different reason. My four year old, Kali, followed Amity singing, "Winkle winkle whittle star. How I wonder what you are . . .

REF

Pool, Robert. Chaos theory, How big an advance?, Science v245:4913 pps 26-28 (1989).

"COLOR ME ORANGE"

This is not about rolling Agent Orange drums for Project Ranch Hands, although I've been splashed; rather, this is about kids grasping from thin air specious straws to fashion their Raft of Wants to launch at you, and their torpedoes of a sort. Or maybe it's about fruit, I don't know. Anyway, my kids could propel a litany of itchy, specious straw rafts. Repetitive recitals of bogus, but superficially legitimate straws for consideration of, say, the purchase of watermelon bubblegum. Then, there is the Appeals Circuit. Like, "Watermelons are good for you!" "No spitting pits Dad, honest!" "Green is GOOD!" "They aren't made of Asbestos" and the itchiest, "Would you rather get us some Twinkies?" I'm not sure if the rash that ensued was from straw or apoplexy, but distinctions about molecular composition or supply shortages kind of worked on me, plus the kids' eyes were like puppy dogs.

Not so when I was a kid, Cocker spaniel eyes and all. Adults short-circuited my invocations. Sank my raft of appeals likened to starvation with an adult-like wisdom, "That's apples and oranges." Said even to, "I'll die without some!" End of conversation. No appeals. Period. Like there was no rhyme or reason to my vision, but what did I know? There wasn't much gum either. The only thing that lasted then was fruitcake around Christmas time. (By Easter even that would be gone.) I diverge . . . Adult wisdom appeared as a nonsequitor.

When you are a small kid you need to be able to run fast, have a PhD in semantics or at least not cry when the World turns dark. I could run, but was captive to Donald Duck comic books, Mickey Mouse programs and had nowhere to run well into the Age of Reason. By then, Existence appeared baked into a collective fruitcake, that everybody bought or made, but few could stomach, unless desperate. But I did learn to read and this fruit thing sure required some study when I realized "fruit" was more than a NYC 42nd Street Fairy no normal kid wanted to emulate. Adults hadn't yet thought of, "Just say, NO" which brings us back to the wisdom that torpedoed my litany of rafts. I.E. Just what in hell do "apples and oranges" have to do with chewing gum?

Well, apples symbol like crazy, mostly Rockwellian images of fertility, abundance and excellence. As in, "the apple of one's eye" or "in apple pie order" and to ward off doctors. The venerated French fry even comes from what they call "Pome de Terre" (apple of the Earth). Lots of other fruits are associated with Apple too. (Yet a pineapple is closer to a potato, but who's criticizing?) Need I mention the "Big Apple"? Citadel of Capitalism, foundation to the ENTIRE Fruitcake. OK, maybe just the oven to our prosperity. Apple pie and mothers go together.

Then, there is this dark side to Apple, like Original Sin; meat from the Tree of Knowledge lodged in Adam's children's children's children's throats. My throat had enough to gag me on Fridays when we were forced to eat fish just because Adam ate a forbidden Apple which didn't seem very fair to me at the time. Why on Friday I don't know . . . I'm kind of guessing here . . . but something sure affects the words of Man with darkness. Apples?

Even Snow White was victimized with an apple whose blood red skin promised darkness. The Apple has been with Man from the beginning of Knowledge. Before the discovery of dirt. The Apple presented Man with his first illusion—nakedness, his first paradox of Existence—The Fortunate Fall. Shame on Apple. (In defense, however, the Apple was not eaten until after Adam and Eve displayed flaws in will and reason, respectively. Shame on Adam and Eve.)

The Apple symbols loudly and variegated beside the relatively silent, but distinctive Orange. The Orange symbols estrangement beside the Apple with its worlds of association. Try rhyming Orange with anything. Orange is out of step with poetic harmony—the underpinning of Existence. Carrots, tigers, pumpkins, Halloween banded together with Orange, but rhyme-less, set apart, alienated, homeless, and mute beside the Apple.

The Orange is my brother. Alienated, but warm. Color me Orange.

Adults were right-on when I was a kid. Not only was I one of the Oranges pleading nonsense for disallowed "Apples", EVERYTHING appeared a dissonant mixture of "apples and oranges" and like fruitcake, didn't make sense then, and doesn't now. Kind of like we are all Oranges in an Apple grove we aren't supposed to eat in, wondering why watermelon gum makes our tongues green and DNA to shorten. This must keep God laughing.

"FLOYD'S FIRST FLAT FROG"

Have you ever ached on a sky blue day? Not from that neurotic anxiety Kermit probably has, but for a flattened frog? Floyd's first at the Hop-In #114 convenient store. That's the day my tea bag broke.

Symbolism is powerful; shit, we live in a world of symbols. The illusion is that we live in an objective world. E.G. One dollar = George Washington and a flat frog is a flat frog. Not so. Everything is symbolic—tealeaves, rainbows, the cross, circles, $, and yes, even "Hop-In" frogs. So they aren't just flattened frogs.

What made Floyd's first flattened frog so interesting, symbolic that is, was the environment in which the frog met its Maker. Leather flat, next to an unleaded gas pump, on top of petroleum-soaked concrete, underneath a, dead, white neon light. What a hell-of-a-way to go. Kind of like going to the hospital. The sky was still blue.

It wasn't natural. I mean, how could this incredibly brave, but stupid frog have crossed all that pavement to arrive at his "spot". In one piece. Kind of laid out like a bearskin rug, only smaller—like a frog. It may not have been Floyd's first. It was a first for the frog.

The symbolism was awesome. Nature meets technology. SPLAT treaded. I wonder how we humans are doing? I wonder who's responsible for tea bags?

The tea leaves symboled in silence from the bottom of my cup as I ached for the stupid frog on a sky blue day.

Why? I did read once that just about the whole human race appears to be born vulnerable to emotional turmoil.*

I know I'm disturbed.

REF

* Ellis, Albert. "Making Ourselves Neurotic." The Humanist, Mar/Apr 1992.

"STILL LIFE"

I tell you this my son,
That some of us are musicians,
Some athletes, some warriors,
Nurturers, gadflies, . . .
I am a loner.
If there are causal agents
For our natures,
God knows,
There are experiences for them.
If by birth, God bless us.
Loners are not empty.
I was born with emotions
In Flatbush
A place which still glows
Of open air markets colorful produce
And autumn leaf piles covering young limbs
With dry crackly smells.
The iron grated stairs of public school.
Angst?

Hope Farm,
A land with no empty bottles
And no returns.
Dormitories the far side of civilization
Counting the new cries
In the homesickness.
The emptiness of Visitor's Day
Louder than the inner
Crumbling of belonging.
One-way run-away
Tickets on commuter rails,
Adolescent binge times,
Until the black-walled cruisers
Inevitably retraced the tracks

Whispering their authority.
Dormitories transformed to barracks,
Angst to fear, boredom, rockets, mortars, drunks
Hatred shining out from dark
Asian eyes impaled on stressed Buddha's.

My fellow bomb men, as close,
Yet as enigmatic as the slant-eyed girl,
Who beat our clothes on the washing rocks,
Shared C-rats, tent, and impervious humor
Coercing fuse wire under the Sun's glare,
Mingling sweat.

The rockets and tracers arched through the night
As liquors spilt under the flare-blinded stars.
The World was indeed a wondrous place.
Somewhere the zest for it waned
And a fog moved in.
The desert swallowed it—
Dreaming places void of footsteps,
Gunfire muted,
The embrace gone from the shattered air.
Sharing . . . the Bean Bandit,
Pineapple, Murphy—
Beaten like a piece of slaughterhouse meat.
All gone somewhere.
Born alone, die alone.
No blame.
It is said we choose our lives.

Now it is your turn.

"HOME IS THROUGH THE WOODS"

Winding down the mountainside as dusk and fog settled in the broken woods scarred with stumps and splintered trees wove a haunting reverie—which ill-prepared me for the explosion of words my oldest girl had "tripped" the entrance door of her friend's house with. I heard the bullet though.

"Hey dad, I found my spirit animal!"

Spirit? "That's nice", I tried to dodge, "What's that?"

"It's a rabbit", Amity said as she hopped around a corner of her friend Cara's darkened briar patch living room. She was so excited, her characteristic 'Hi Dad' became a casualty in our social lubrication, but she did a good jump-hug, kathunk, into my chest. "Isn't that great Dad?"

I guessed it was. I don't know. Spirit? Isn't that the idea of the brain? (Great idea brain.) I wondered who thought of "mind" first. I wondered who sold the first piece of land. I wondered who bought it. Some ideas are like bullets to the foot. Ideas like more and bigger bullets for one.

"How did you find it Amity? I'd like to hear this", was heartfelt enough, considering her bullet wasn't the first of that caliber tonight. My mood had been shot to shit. The mountain road, a gun barrel coil through a ravaged wood memorial to War Zone D or Hill 881, had not invited anything but mental bullets, some of which were already in permanent residence. The man-sheared, crater-pocked slope a vivid testimony to mans' madness or somebody's. I guess that's why I thought of Hill 881. Just who are we? Surely not rabbits.

Getting my daughters' presence and belongings unglued from friends who acted as if they hadn't seen anyone for three hundred years wasn't too hard, although we forgot a roller skate and winter coat. Both Amity's. Getting my presence out of this swelling brain hole to the past was proving a lot harder.

Hill 881, you know, like most every other hill in Vietnam was devastated. But that's not what made it remarkable. What made Hill 881 remarkable was that on a 1967 May Day many of the dead were found lying next to their M-16s broken down in the act of repairing them. Why do you think that was? Why do I feel guilty? We were going uphill now.

"I found it in a hole", Amity continued.

"What?" Oh yeah, the rabbit. "You're kidding!" I say.

Kali was silent. She accepted a lot at 6 years old. Amity, at 8, was apparently old enough to take a vision quest. Through a hole, no less. Which was what the almost nonexistent road looked like. Only the shoulders remained, the rest having been eaten by fog. If it got any thicker we would be driving by sound.

"No, really Dad. I did." she testified, "The woman's' group beat a drum and I visualized a hole in a waterfall and went in. Kali's too young", she concluded.

"Am not!" Kali enjoined.

"Are too!"

"Not."

"Too."

"No you're not Kali. The women said I was old enough. Not you."

"Well Kali's got a spirit animal too, Am. What happened when you went through the waterfall? And what kind of hole is that?—a waterfall?"

"Yeah, really Dad. I thought of this hole that went right through a waterfall, all lined with flowers."

The road was going to be lined with our parts if I couldn't see any better. Kali, suspecting the same blurted, "Hey Dad, how can you see?"

Good question, I thought, but out came, "I drive by sound Kali." Making me wonder whose in charge here. To compensate I added, "You know, like listen for the sound of gravel on the side of the road, the sound of dead Hardee bags, beer cans, deer, anything is a clue in the fog."

"No you don't", she said, ... Do you?"

"Nah", I confessed, "I just remember the way the road goes, follow the shoulder and so I can tell where we are." You have to have faith—giggled from somewhere in my brain—you know, like the road actually continued beyond the gray wall two feet in front of the truck. Only the shoulder moved. It was a still fog.

The dash lights lit us up like radium dials, so while, fortunately, we still existed in this fog, we looked altered in some strange way.

That's what got them on Hill 881—alterations. Alterations by a few good men and in this case—the good men designing Army weapons under the tenets of good wound ballistics. With all this goodness, you would have thought the military a good place to be. It was and it wasn't, that's another story, but for sure, they didn't use good weapons ballistics.

We stilled glowed radium-white like termite people on the outbound moon shuttle. The girls didn't mention it, probably because they were listening for gravel sounds or metal bending. Not really. This was my gallows humor and me. I tried not to bullshit them on serious matters.

Amity wasn't concerned. She was into describing the flowers that lined the waterfall hole—all around, top and bottom, the entire length and plop—she tumbled out into a field of clover. A big field. With nothing but clover. The field was empty. The sky was clear blue, the sun—golden warm. A real peaceful place.

"So what happened?" I said, "How come there wasn't any animal there?"

"I don't know", she replied, "But I had this incredible urge to fly. So I did. High into the air and all around to the wooded edge and I twirled and twisted in the sky. It was so much fun!"

'God', I thought, it sounds like astral travel. Psychic stuff. I heard people get stuck on the astral plane, wherever that is.

"I came back", she said, "and there was a rabbit there. Eating."

"Wow", I breathed, "A rabbit."

The fog opened up a little, giving back some 20 feet of pavement and some black White Pine limbs. Give me my life back fog, came from somewhere—just a thought. I wasn't impressed with the rabbit.

"What makes you think it was your spirit animal?" I asked.

"The women say that if you visualize going through a hole, you know, while they beat a drum, then you might meet your spirit animal."

. . . . The silence was deafening in its timelessness.

"Or you might not", she concluded, "But I did."

The fog closed in and the black White Pine disappeared. We were alone again.

"What's your spirit animal Dad?" Kali broke in.

"I don't know if I have a spirit animal Kal." And I don't want to bullshit you either, I thought. What to do? What to do?

"So what happened while you were in the field Amity?", I feinted.

"Well, it was really nice Dad. The rabbit just ate there quietly and then another rabbit came and another and another. There were lots of rabbits all of a sudden. I LOVE rabbits!"

People eat rabbits. Now I won't be able to. If I had to, I'd rather trap rabbits for food, than shoot deer or eat food stamps. Why couldn't she be a squirrel or a raccoon? Why a rabbit? Of course people shoot all three—so what the hey.

"So, what color were they?"

"White."

"All of them? Not any brown or gray ones?"

"Yep, all white", she fondly cooed.

With red eyes too, I mused. Spooky looking rabbits those albinos. Small and soft, but kind of disturbing never the less. Just like this hill and spirit business.

"So what's your spirit animal Dad?" Kali persisted. She was into one compass heading. Steady as she goes, like she is the Queen Mary and you—one tugboat.

"Well, I haven't exactly found my spirit animal yet Kali." As a matter of fact, I don't even know if I have a spirit, other than "chicken", but the idea is certainly more appealing than dust-to-dust pronouncements or dead battery landfill analogies. "I wish I had one", I compromised.

"Everyone's got one Dad", comforted Amity, "Because you have a spirit", unknowingly begging the question.

"They all go to Heaven when you die", Kali notes matter of factly.

"No they don't", says Amity.

"Do to!"

"Don't."

"Do."

"No they don't Kali, some stay."

"NAH HUH. THEY GO TO HEAVEN", Kali shouts.

"There's ghosts", Amity explains.

Silence in the truck. The wiper blades are going—thunk, thunk, thunk—and the gray fog signals—nothing.

"Well not in this country", Kali triumphantly announces, "They aren't allowed here."

I'm thinking, both these kids know how to pull rabbits out of the hat.

"Yeah, really Kal", I said, "Who wants ghosts around here anyway? They have laws against that. They have laws for everything—seatbelts, the price of lettuce, ghosts."

Amity contradicts with a skeptical, "Sure Dad."

Which I won't pass.

"Amity, did you know that the condensed version of the Ten Commandments has around twenty-six words in it and the federal guidelines for pricing a head of lettuce has over fifteen thousand words. Trust me, we have laws for everything Am." No wonder we are all bad. It's a litigious certainty.

"So what happened while you were there with all the rabbits Am? Did you have a nice time?" Ghosts weren't for Kali, rabbits were. Kali cried for a week when she found out the Chinese ate cats.

Amity sighed, "Yeah we did Dad." Like you could tell Amity loves rabbits. "But then some squares with animals in them came", she added.

"Squares with animals?"

. . . And they were closing in which was kind of scary."

"Yeah, I bet. What kind of animals were they?", I asked, "and were they in cubes or were they flat two-dimensional things?"

"Well", Amity responded, "They were like in TV screens—so they were flat, but they were still scary because they kept closing in more and more. One was a horse and one was a bear."

"Hmmm", I said, "So what did you do?"

"I said, 'HELP' and all the rabbits ate the squares up."

"Just like that!", I mimicked her astonishment.

"Yeah, just like that! It was great Dad. Then everything was just like it was. The squares didn't come back."

Hmmm, the squares never left, if you are what you eat.

Whoa. The county trash bins suddenly appeared as green squares to emphasize nothing or everything is coincidentally related. I knew the squares were really cubes for refuse—that place where all the cans, bottles and Hardee bags in the ditches didn't go.

The mountainside appeared again as 881—stumps, snapped trees and a clinging fog much like the classic graveyard shift. I'm sure the girls noticed with their furtive glances over the slope, but for the most part, they kept their eyes fixated into the moon—fog shrouded over the dash. They were spooked by the thought of ghosts like all kids were. I know I was haunted.

"Dad! Dad! Dad!", they yelled as we disappeared in a sharp left away from the green cubes and the moon.

"Do you hear any gravel?", I assured them, "Don't worry, the road goes left here, then sharp right, then straight a bit, and right and right and we're right on top—watch."

I threw in a lot of 'rights' because they are positive words and who's counting after awhile? Kali was uncharacteristically silent. Like she was still thinking of ghosts or something. Who needs ghosts? That's what memories are—ghosts of the past. And visions—ghosts of the future. All are in the present, as we exist in all three worlds simultaneously—unless you are feeble-minded or brain dead.

That's what the Army was—feeble-minded, when they decided to alter the AR-15. A proven assault rifle with virtually no jams was declared to be inadequate. They wanted a bigger, faster spinning bullet with a higher rate of fire. They achieved this with a new rifling and slow burning powder. The M-16 was born. The proof to their ingenuity was Hill 881. Defoliated, Napalmed and the end of over one hundred men one day in May—most of whom were found dead trying to repair their jammed rifles from the residual effects of slow burning powder (1). This is what I hear. A good rifle was wasted on me.

That was Hill 881 and the slope tonight reminded me of that waste. I don't know why as slopes like this look simply Napalmed after the loggers leave.

The fog was gone and we were on top of the mountain. No ice yet as I sped up so we could get back and let Ren the puppy out. (He was a ten-week-old pit bull who still seemed to pee wherever he wanted to, but I was worried about what he was chewing on more so than my spirit, now that I saw the way home. The ghosts were behind us, figuratively speaking, home was ahead.

"So. How did you leave Amity?" I was back with her.

"It was easy. Like floating. Right through the hole and I brought all the rabbits back."

"All of them?"

"Yep", beaming, "All of them."

"Can we eat one if we are hungry?" I tried.

"No, it's against the law."

"What about bad guys? Communist rabbits with red eyes."

"No guys are bad Dad. They just do bad things."

"Maybe so Am." But why can't I tell the difference?

"Here's our road Dad!", Kali proudly noted. She liked being navigator and is good about finding her way home. She should be. Her Indian name symbols, "The Ferry Across The Ocean Of Existence."

She says we are ALL going to Heaven.

REF

"The M-16 was strongly defended as a fine assault rifle, and Army officers in both Saigon and Washington suggested in private that Marine carelessness in training and maintenance had been responsible for its breakdown in battle. Then, on the other side of the world, Congressman James J. Howard of New Jersey (rose to) the floor of the House of Representatives to read a letter from a bitter Marine who had been wounded in the Hill Fights warning his parents not to believe what they read in the newspapers. "We left with 250 men in our company and came back with 107. Practically every one of our dead was found with his rifle torn down next to him . . . (By) January, 1968 . . . all the M-16s in Vietnam had been recalled, refitted with chrome chambers and a new buffer system to reduce the rate of fire, and provided with a different gunpowder to lessen jamming." http://members.networld.com/mje1/barrydon/hill_fights.htm

"LAUNDRY TIME"

"As far as the laws of mathematics refer to reality, they are not certain;
as far as they are certain, they do not refer to reality"

Albert Einstein

After the beginning of Time there was laundry. Notice I didn't say at the beginning of Time or before the beginning, because we (and I use that term loosely) can't determine the conditions of the Universe before 10 to the minus 43rd power of a second. I.E. before 0.000000000000000000000000 00000000000000000001th of a second after its origin. Who knows if there was laundry in that speck of time? Anyway, the math doesn't rewind back to Zero. (A math fly in the reductionistic ointment of science.) Something happened in that speck of Time and it apparently bothered Einstein , but this is about laundry, the incredible mass of it that needs to be dealt with, and disappearing socks about 12 billion years after the Big Bang.

I just did two hours worth of laundry, which is worse than ponderous given, I just told you, the entire Universe was formed in less than 10 to the minus 43rd power of a second and then expanded, but I didn't tell you this—like my laundry pile. Washed two loads, folded yesterday's laundry—in which I found just two socks for Moi, not much, but at least they were paired. 'Am I not contributing to the pile in the bathroom?' I think to myself. Maybe I am unconsciously trying to lighten the load by obsessively keeping my current garb clean? Whatever. Obsession has no impact on reducing the mass of clothes piled almost organically in the bathroom. Two hours didn't make an impression.

I swear (no help), there may even be two piles in the bathroom, but they are so close together it is a moot question. The mass seems to be growing. I know it's maybe a tic in my eye. I mean, really—three kids. Still, I'm wondering with all that weight and time if the mass could be regenerating in some quantum way . . . No! That's idiotic. More than likely the bottom of the laundry pile is being compressed into a Black Hole—which is really not a hole any more than a bowling bowl is, but you know what I mean.

Einstein said that Black Holes could be a bridge to another Universe, since there is so much force exerted at the center as to theoretically squeeze matter out of Existence. He also said space was like a sheet spread out, only bigger. Put some bowling balls on it here and there and you'll see contoured depressions spiking out from the balls sunken now a little in space. The "Sheet" theory is seconded by modern physics as the Big Bang is now considered to have originated as a single point (which conceptually has no size dimensions) that expanded into a featureless elastic sheet—a continuum in which the point is the same everywhere—a "point of order" if you will.

I used to think Gravity wasn't a force so much as that of a situation in which matter (socks in this case) was being caught as it rolled by that contoured depression leading toward the bowling ball. Kind of like a pea falling into a slot at Monte Carlo. So a sock, for example, can simply lay around until kicked into one of these invisible depressions in the fabric of space and wind up a member of the mass with the longest or deepest depression (a Black Hole). There must be one in every bathroom. There's one in every Galaxy.

Those are theories. I know my socks are not being crushed out of Existence. Well, maybe a sock or two may be. Just a suspicion. You know how that goes.

I swear (yet again) that the laundry IS growing into a Black Hole—attracting more and more clothes, faster and faster, reaching out further and further. Eureka! I realize some of Kali, Amity or Zach's friends left clothes here. And maybe the two similar-sized neighborhood boys too. A plethora of kids seem to gravitate here. What? I'm the only parent that doesn't beat their kids? Dubious. I suspect a Black Hole in the bathroom.

I think I'm on to something here.

What a bummer I don't have the mental teeth to gnaw on this any longer, but the physical realities of laundry require attention in other areas as well—like attention to your weapons. Today, fortunately, my Sears Heavy Duty friend of 21 years, who has been resurrected a few times and coaxed with the usual arsenal of hammers and screwdrivers, many, made it through the cycles without the usual valve-sticking, filter clogged, timer brownout, belt-slipping, death rattle spin. There's nothing like a good washing machine. If you could get anything through "the eye of the needle" on the path to Heaven—you'd bring a good washing machine. I figure, if a camel can get through that smaller portal next to the main gate (the "eye of a needle") by just stooping a little, surely my friend here is coming with me. At least Kali says we are all going to Heaven I digress.

Some of the two hours was spent folding and putting away, but I don't really angst about this put away stuff as much as the kids hear it. Concern is an atmosphere created for the kids who don't understand Chaos Theory. See, folding androgynous clothes that are all too big for their proper owners, but just right for the Pop culture (Slacker at this point), means that I don't have the foggiest idea as to whose laundry is whose. Aristotle's wife couldn't figure it out, so I rely on Chaos to provide a non-linear path to the proper owners. You see, Chaos mediates the zone between random placement and strict determinism. The Theory implies or suggests that, although not in a straight line, the proper clothes will be "attracted" in some "strange" way to the proper kids. I think it works, but not altogether with socks.

Logic can not explain it. Logic is a poor model of the Universe. For example, logic can try to describe the electro-magnetic motor of my Sears washing machine as an alternating current forcing the motor to rotate by switching from one pole (P1) to another pole (P2) rapidly. This stated in a logical syllogism, gives us:

If P1: Then Not P1.

If P2: Then Not P2.

Now that's descriptive, but not helpful. The logic of Cycle On = Machine On and Cycle Off = Machine Off should work as well, but my Sears washing machine doesn't give a damn about any stinking cycles logic. It has a mind of it's own and it's short some circuits like some people are. No offense intended.

Two hours of laundry. I wonder if this laundry time stuff has anything to do with perpetual motion?

"REALITY CHECK"

I'm not paranoid. But you know that doesn't mean they're not out to get you. Or maybe they have already and they're just checking. Anyway, when I got home Amity told me there was a message on the answering machine from the Salem Veterans Hospital.

Meaning she must have been sleeping when they called, because no phone goes unanswered with teenagers in the house. But then the dishes were all cleaned, rugs vacuumed and she had made a cherry pie. What a daughter. I guess blowing up yesterday did make an impression. The pie was still warm. So maybe she slept late and went like a whirlwind a couple of hours before I got home. I didn't ask. We talked about making the pie. She really made a fine looking example. Too bad I told her 1 Tblsp of salt instead of 1 tsp. Too much poison gas, too much poison metal. It makes a difference you know. We laughed.

The message was kind of salt on old memories. The VA wants a bone scan. You know the routine bone scan vets get who coexisted with Agent Orange (AO). I've got a bridge to sell if you believe that. The VA and DODS denied AO was responsible for anything until recently even though they suspected back in 1965 that there were possibly carcinogenic outcomes. (That's when prisoners at Holmesburg State Prison in Philadelphia were subjected to dioxin, the highly toxic component of AO and studied by the Government for the development of cancer.) And that's when we started dumping more than 11 million gallons in Vietnam, which followed Agents Purple (2,4-D;2,4,5-T), Blue (Phytar 560-G/ Cacodylic acid), Pink (2,4.5-T), Green (2,4,5-T), and White (Tordon 101/2,4-D; picloram).

I'm sure they would bury everyone like they buried the MIAs and POWs if they could. Vets are an embarrassment, a political liability, and lack the good grace to die. As Col. Peck stated when he resigned from his DIA post as Chief of the Special Office for Prisoners of War and Missing in Action (POW-MIA), "Everyone is expendable. I have seen firsthand how ready and willing the policy people are to sacrifice or 'abandon' anyone who might be perceived as a political liability. It is quick and facile, and can be easily covered." But we are still here and can't be swept away that easily.

Now you can get compensation for prostrate cancer if you aren't already dead from the other possible cancers. Like maybe $5 a month to maintain an inflatable doughnut for your impotent ass or whatever in. So I called back and asked, "Why me? What are my last four? And do you think I should be paranoid?"

The nurse responded, "Because a doctor in Oncology ordered it. Eight-four-eight-three. (And) I would be, but don't worry we'll straighten this out."

I think now, maybe they want to steal-a-bone or something. The Chinese are doing it. You know, "Gee Mr. Stuvwxyz what could have happened to your tibia? It was here a minute ago! What's that? Your left femur is missing too? And I thought the sheet made your leg look like a noodle. Forgive me, we'll get right on this. Can you describe your femur? Somebody is going to pay for this . . . Like an orderly will be sent to a VA hospital in North Dakota for a year to ten.

Who would be nuts enough to go to a VA Nuclear Medicine Dept. because of some oncologist who doesn't know you from an alligator suitcase? Maybe it was a competency test. I don't know. Not oriented x three. Off you go. Or they're offering free bone scans to vets with arrest warrants on them. Off you go. I don't know. Usually you have to beg or crawl to get in. At a minimum, you can't be a pain-in-the-ass. Now they are calling. Hmmmm.

Can you get some Percacets with a bone scan?—I wonder—as I get lots of cherries and just a wee, tiny bit of crust. Life is good.

"THE SALEM FROG TRIALS"

The sun was a giant red ball lumbering upwards in its early launch from the horizon. My headlights were on as were everyone else's on I-81, except for the occasional maniac. But aside from the headlights and giant sun, the visibility was ethereal, a shadow world of monochrome forms going north and south to whatever—somewhere in between dust-to-dust I thought. The sun is always there. It looms over our dust.

I feel an affinity to the sun at these times—to Andromeda, the wind, dust. To Existence. The observer observing living. And yep, I'm alive pinch me and so's the sun. I love the state of just simply existing. Some call me a couch potato, but how else can you pay attention to the wind and sun or listen to the grass grow? Or even just simply exist? If we were all couch potatoes there wouldn't be war, but somewhere in between dust-to-dust monochrome forms ideate purpose. Spiritual theories. Social theories. Economic.

I wondered what "existence" after death would be like with no sense of self, the personality destroyed in furtherance of the Plan as the Esoterics claim. Just awareness of "belonging" maybe. On the surface this seems better than Mark Twain's heaven, but can you appreciate "existence" with no personality? Dubious. Let's be real. After all, it's the brain's "idea"—all this mind, spirit, unconscious business and when the brain goes . . . It ain't "being" anymore. It's dead. And the body isn't being anymore. Tell me you haven't felt some alteration around dead "beings" like something is dissociated. No wonder Christians refuse to die.

God, death and dying. Monochrome forms, all under a giant red sun I wished I could enjoy. But going to the hospital on what could be a sky-blue day was too much like Floyd's First Flat Frog arriving at "his" spot under a dead white neon light—and I don't know anymore than him, except maybe that God wears tire tread sandals. And me with the gift of thought, think I could be Floyd's second, because I, like the frog, didn't know where I was going.

I didn't know which exit to take, but got there anyway—went the wrong way on a one way and a wrong turn and arrived at the cement basement of Building 2 wondering about frogs, existence, belonging, coffee and doughnuts. I was at the X-Ray Department telling the clerk that I could "eat a chair". She acted like I was from Mars, not realizing I was recently in touch with my related matter (carbon) on Andromeda. So I forgave her mainstream "being" Earth time. It's important to get in touch with the reality of the day, like where you are, in between "dust-to-dust". Otherwise they lock you up.

A young technician prepared me for the IVP. Pink gown, no buttons on the underwear, no letters or cryptic messages on the T-shirt. Pink gown?

"Don't you have blue?"

"Green?"

Pink, that's it and cut to fit someone that looks like a horseshoe. Like the old vets slumped over in their wheelchairs. So we are discussing the possibility of kidney failure, toxic reactions, levels of radiation and I'm in a pink gown.

All positioned to be injected with radioactive iodine, I popped my head up and said, "What if I really don't need to be here?"

"I mean, the nurse in the clinic spilled all the urine and ten minutes latter the doctor goes—there's blood in my urine." (I didn't tell her that the nurse wiped it all up with brown paper towels, no gloves, just like a fast food chain.) I go on.

"Maybe it's not my blood in the urine."

"Maybe it's not my urine."

"The clinic was like a fast food chain."

"Maybe they got the wrong urine."

"That's not why I'm here!"

"I'm here for something else!"

"OK go ahead."

What do I know? I don't think she ever said a word.

A doctor with a strong NYC accent and wiry black hair tells me to expect a "stick" or maybe a "mosquito". So when it goes in feeling like a knife, I say, "More like a New Jersey mosquito."

And he asks, "Oh yeah, where in Jersey are you from?"

"Spent time in Newark", I respond.

"I'm from Brooklyn, you can tell." He was born in Brooklyn, but was schooled on the Eastside of Manhattan. "And we all know what that's like", he finishes.

Like we are Homeboys I suppose. I didn't think he ever worried about being shoved in front of a subway. (They'd want his credit cards.) I used to worry, but just because you are fearful, doesn't mean you won't be shoved in front of one. I told him instead, there's hope for his accent, because I was born in Brooklyn and mine's gone. He stabbed me in the arm as a final adjustment.

Like we are all homeboys, I suppose. I didn't think he ever worried about being shoved in front of a subway. (They'd want his credit cards.) I used to worry and just because you are fearful, doesn't mean you won't be shoved in front of an onrushing subway. I told him instead, there's hope for his accent, because I was born in Brooklyn too and mine is gone. He stabbed me in the arm as a final adjustment.

"Are you OK?", everyone asks periodically, as the young technician pushes iodine up my vein. I'm feeling weird. Like I'm suffocating in the body of a stranger. My cheeks are flushing, my taste buds are signaling caulk or something and this young technician is pushing iodine into my organs.

"OK", I say, because if I talk I'll puke.

The older technician with grey in her hair touched a lot as if she didn't know where my body was under the gown. She said that if the solution goes through fast then the pictures would be taken fast. But sometimes the solution went through the system slowly and the wait could be longer. I waited, picturing little radioactive iodine balls bouncing and careening into everything, insides glowing.

I didn't care. Everyone was attentive to me albeit to see if my kidneys failed or something. Earlier the young technician said she hadn't seen one fail. That the consent/awareness form was just procedure, but she could have started last week for all I know. I was marveling about this technology aimed at my abdomen and of course the older tech's mothering. The bolts holding the machine to the wall were as big as my fists. Specially made. And I the recipient by virtue of being a veteran. Good deal.

I was asked to pee before the final series of pictures and was smiling broadly as I pushed back through the lavatory door—like the door was a test and I beat it. Hungry enough to eat a chair and I made it back through the door that would have entombed an older vet. So I must have passed some kind of test. The pictures continued.

"How come you took so many pictures?", I asked the young technician with maybe a weeks experience. Surely I can get something out of her. She seemed honestly naive.

"Well your kidneys are higher than we thought", she responds.

'High kidneys?' What does that mean? Longer tubes that's for sure. So what, everyone's different. Who's normal?

When the older technician bounced back saying, "How are you doing?", again, I asked whether the solution went through slow or fast. Like was it bouncing into things? She says the solution went through like through a normal person. What's normal? I think it's normal to die. And when everyone with memories of you is dead, then you are really dead.

Well, I didn't have kidney failure or anything and the young technician said I was great patient as she escorted me to the X-Ray waiting area for an

ultrasound of why I really came to the hospital for months ago. She also
said there wasn't time for coffee or doughnuts, wherever they were.

Whoever gets a mass in their epididymis? It's not normal. I felt like a frog.
Dressed in pink gown, watching WWI vets in wheelchairs, a WWII type
with thick glasses unpacking a thicker book well worn with posters or
pictures pasted into it, and a somewhere in between me and the last ten
years—a black bearded, long haired guy with a small hole in the right breast
of his flannel shirt. We all looked like bums, except I was in a pink gown
like the older vets—watching his used Styrofoam cup of coffee—wondering
where he got it.

The flannel shirted vet's hand and foot started to tremble like some
extrapyramidal effect of psychotropics. Then they would stop. He was
definitely screwed up. I wondered if we weren't all screwed up. My boot laces
weren't even tied and I sat there in a pink gown with a mass on my testicle. I've
come a long way to here, I think. So I tried to be "aware" of where here was.
Starting with fingers pressed together for that touch of "hereness". I heard
everything. The flannel shirted limb and black socks collapsed were twitching
again signaling his history as the old guys slumped their total histories into
their wheelchairs. I bet we were all in some wild shit far aways places doing
wild shit once. Now we were here, amidst the X-Ray admissions counter,
florescent lights and environmental babble of a subterranean hospital. Like a
frog would go to. "Pith me" "Pith me", we all cried.

"Mr. Stuvwxyz" "Mr. Stuvwxyz", a male voice calls me into a narrow more
focused "being here". Like it is happening to me now. I follow thinking I
knew a male would be involved with my testicle. Since he has to hold the
ultrasound thing against my thing, he asks out of the side-of-his-mouth, in a
whisper, eyes furtively nailing the door, "Is it in your right uhmm . . . ball?"
Like no shit, a ball, what a bummer.

I qualify it with a "Nah, it's in my epididymis"—like alien-in-my-chest
or something, but I'm a lot more cavalier about it. Since I'm not sure he
knows what the epididymis is any more than I do—everything seemed
better.

Well, a Dr. Selby came looking at my testicle and friend on the B&W screen.
This star trek glow irradiated her face and another woman's, the sonogram

technician whatever. She kept adjusting "translateral" and something like on a submarine with the male technician.

"How old is he?", asks the glowing doctor from the corner of my eye. (God forbid she ask me.)

"49"

Yeah well, 49 plus the mass equals what? "So what do you think it looks like?", I ask. Her kind of pretty face doesn't move under her wire glasses and both women continue to stare at the screen basking them with a lunar landscape of right testicle et al.

"Wait here like you are Mr. Dewey" and the lights whip on coloring my pink gown and my boot tips hanging over the end of the table. Everyone was in the hall and my boxer shorts were still around my knees. It was over, but it wasn't. Just like everything else was in the air. After awhile someone popped a head in that told me to dress. Goodbye pink gown. Hello clothes. I can see this mass, my mass, on the screen below your truly's name. There were black areas and white areas. Yep, something there alright. I knew there would be.

The two women are in the hall maybe conniving some feminist shit as I exit the room in my Harly Davidson hat. "So, what's it look like?", I bounce over to them.

"Get in touch with your doctor" dribbles back from their huddle on the hall wall.

They looked like I didn't want to know. If you know what I mean. I still didn't know shit. And so, hopped back home, back to my pond the far side of nowhere. Where things pretty much "is" and the sun comes up sometimes, because it's supposed to.

Thunk! . . . The kids gawked at me as the basketball slowly bellied-up like a dead cow. An arrow shaft, dead center in it's pinkness, pointing the way toward basketball heaven. How could I shoot my faithful and longtime ball! Incredible. Like shooting yourself in the foot, but worse. Your foot could heal. It was that kind of week.

Dad's now dead basketball symboled primal messages about cause and effect to the kids now surrounding it's last sigh. Their eyes intensively switching from my reaction to the obvious and traumatic "deadness" of my beloved ball. I took it well and would bury it where Quest the Shepard who actually ate my 1970's ball lay. What a bite she had! She ate rocks, basketballs, rugs, door jambs . . . canine oral fixation . . . It was her fatal flaw. She even tried to eat the postman's car door while he was moving. It was her last fixation.

Dead basketballs, dead animals, dead sky. What a hell-of-a-spring. And I had to go back to the Salem VA again. Another reality check.

When I did get to the Med/Surg Clinic in the soon-to-be-dead Bldg. 12 for my 3 o'clock appointment, which I discovered the other 40 guys to have as well—I thought the nurse said, "You're just in time." And I was I brightly thought, 3 pm, but she actually said, "My shoes just untied." And sure as shit they were. Sorry white laces dragging their limp forms behind her scuffed white shoes. I knew I would be here forever. As usual, the hallway and waiting room were filled with coughing, slouched vets.

Beside me, I think, was a professional patient another vet who kept saying, "That ain't my name" when the nurse called out names. Across from us was another wall of vets waiting for "Dr. Gaudet", noticeably a guy with no nose—Geez and not even a gauze wad under the bandage. What a way to go I thought. Since he checked in with me I knew we would be together for awhile. So what in the hell are the Emily Post guidelines for addressing a guy with no nose? Nice day for the weather, sorry about your nose. No, that wouldn't be it. Sorry about your nose, nice day for the weather. No, that wouldn't be it either. What a hell of a world.

It was a shitty overcast day, just like the last three months of gloom. I picked up my Parabola magazine on labyrinths. That's what this was—the big freaking waiting room in the bigger cloudy labyrinth. All one had to do is get through, preferably with all your parts. The professional patient kept looking at the cryptic myth and tradition symboling madly from my open magazine, in between his banter with "That ain't my name" and a lady who owned two radio stations and a WWI vet who looked totally incongruous under a brand new baseball hat. (Her father was next to her—the radio stations were who knows where?)

The reason I thought he was a professional patient was because I'd seen him here before and there just were too many vets seeking treatment for one to consistently be there at the same time as yourself. I think he liked the conversation. This time he was talking biblical stuff about God promising this and Jesus that. I wondered how he felt about Genesis 1:29—Where God gives man all the green herbs for his use. Like in pot. So promises are promises and your word is your word. Right. I started writing about dead basketballs and noses. As if I would forget. "That ain't my name" said, "That ain't my name" and I knew he wouldn't forget either.

One of the medical file jackets next to mine had a big green POW stamped on it. I imagined that was his. It could have been the guy with no nose's. He looked depressed as loose shit. My jacket has a category A stamped on it which means "poor as shit" and a Vietnam era DD214 inside which symbols "dumb as shit" or potentially crazed, whichever comes to mind first.

When I met with Dr. Bushman, he seemed as puzzled as I. Like what am I doing here? Then he remembered. "Oh! Don't worry about the mass. It's a neoplastic . . . (something)." What, me worry?

So he still wants a look inside and wants me to pick a date in July. Of course I view this as a "Please cut off my arm" statement, responding, "I can't pick a date—I'm not sure that I want to know." I'm not sure the VA wants to know either. There was Agent Orange and of course, unknown to the general public, Agents White and Blue. And naphtha powder, tritonal, PETN, TNT, comp C, cordite, black powder . . . many glycerines. When mixed with alcohol cause hypotension—and I thought I used to get dizzy from the alcohol. Go figure. Anyway, there could be more chemicals in me than at DuPont and Dow. I could be dead already—prostate cancer et al—I guess that's why Dr. Bushman was concerned. Blood . . . chemicals . . . hmmm.

So he picked a date, gleefully almost. Geez, and who is going to do it I ask the nurse, "Dr. Chainsaw?" (That's what it looked like without my glasses.) She just laughed.

Geez, what a week . . .

It doesn't matter when you go to Roanoke. When you go in the morning the sun is red, the mist thick in the hollows and the abysmal fog—a portal from the far-side-of-nowhere to the "world" as you know it. Absurdity.

Dropping Zachary off at his part job and getting to the Day Hospital at 8 am sharp without coffee was a rush. I had a headache by 8:01. "Didn't they tell you the OR was moved to Friday?", the astonished clerk asks. "Can you come back Friday?", she continues as my affect and headache slump to the floor.

"I'm not coming back."

More astonishment.

"This was Dr. Bushman's idea, not mine. I didn't even pick the date."

The floor nurse then told me of her sister, 40 something, who didn't check up on a lump in her breast and consequently died. I saw the pain in her eyes and didn't ask if there were kids. Maybe there were. Maybe she didn't care to be "here" and was willing to let Nature carry out the inevitable sentence. Maybe she didn't even know why we are here. I sure don't, but figure if there is a Plan to this Life, it's a stupid, freaking Plan.

Or maybe, like Alec Floyd wrote, if there is meaning to this dying, then we need to come back and find it, and then kill it so we don't have to come back again . (The Long War Dead, 1970s). What comes back anyway? What could come back after annihilating my present "Being", my feelings, my awareness, my memories, my consciousness? I ought to be annihilated? Me? What to hell kind of meaning is that?

Well, they got Dr. Sawchuck to do the operation around 2:30. At first, they said Dr. Bushman would do it which would have been good for me as I'm his patient you know. At least it wasn't a Dr. Chainsaw. I have enough anxiety.

Since I had to get blood work and x-rays too, I thought I'd pop into the Psychology Department to see if anyone wanted to talk about existential angst. Dr. Leahe did. You don't want to talk with psychiatrists because all they want is to push psychotropics into the subterranean depths Freud claims is there. To hell with whether or not your beliefs or values preclude "adjustment" on a rational plane. Psychologists at least focus on the healthy superstructure. Sometimes. Most are Behaviorists who think Pavlov's dogs would actually eat the bell and "thought" is some kind of "ghost" in the machine. I stopped thinking this way because my feet wanted to go back, the lower reptilian brain frightened by the neocortex ghost.

I started thinking of Portnoy's Complaint where the doctor goes, "Shall we begin?" That ending is fraught with meaning. And that's why I headed for Dr. Leahe's office. That and a feeling I'm going to explode or something is.

"Yeah, I'm having anxiety attacks. But then, I'm anxious. There's no meaning to any of this. Joseph Campbell said the only meaning was to live it—the existential condition—what the hell kind of meaning is that? My kids give me meaning, but not the "why" of Existence. And I'm not sure if anyone cares and those that seem to, believe in magical notions and animism too. I'm isolated, alienated, depressed, labile, anxious, angry, guilt-ridden and about to pop."

'Next of kin?' was my old response to stressed out veterans at the Albany VA. Dr. Leahe, being more professional at the expense of humor, responded. "How many times have you had the attacks?"

"Well, two recently."

"Would you take medication?" He asks.

"Noooooo, you take yours and I'll take mine" , I responded rather disappointed, adding that I was familiar with the VA psychiatric policy—treat everything as an adjustment disorder or schizophrenia or manic depression or, hey, let's just give everyone psychotropics.

"Not anymore", says Dr. Leahe, "Would you join my PTSD group?"

"That's history", I blurt, "I'm not interested in war stories, adjustment to society or 'supporting' my condition. I want to get better. I'm concerned about my presence here. My Being, my freaking existence."

"You'd be surprised how many people feel like you", Dr. Leahe says, "How about coming to see me next week at 1:30?" Adding, "Is that too soon?"

Too soon for what? Not the Day Hospital. When I got back they'd been looking an hour for me. Getting ready took longer than the flight to OR.

"Hurry, hurry, hurry!" they exclaimed. But what do I know of hospital gowns with only one side, velcro and straps going every which way?

"Oh." "my." "God.", one nurse valley's, as my bare butt and parts flash from the loose gown.

"Try and think like a woman", the other nurse smiles. Chagrin, I thought I was in a hospital.

"Keep your legs together!" they both chortle as I situate on the chair. Geez, this was hard being a woman.

The right front wheel on the chair started vibrating violently around 30 mph, but the nurse laughed and said it ran better like that. She had a 6th sense too. We cut the left turns so tight she HAD to have one—or nobody ever returned from OR. I voted silently for the first.

"You're flashing!"

"Oh." "My." "God.", I valley.

We got there and she was still singing bubbly banter as the tires caught up smoking rubber. And we waited. Truly like coming Home. Hurry up and wait. Everyone learns that from day one, with those memorable words, "Off the bus you Maggots!"

My favorite nurse from the Med/Surg Clinic was here, prepping me. She has an earthy, realness to her. An expertise and matter-of-fact humor that eased your anxiety. At least mine. She asked if I wanted my penis stretched for my wife, but I declined without adding my rhetorical 'What wife?'

"It's been stretched enough with three kids", I state.

Eyes smile while mouths hide behind surgical masks of gauze. One ventriloquist was looking at my DD214.

"Explosives Operator!" he exclaims, "There wasn't much use for you after the service."

"Tell me", I say.

Dr. Sawchuck was young. I may have saw him last week playing in a sandbox. I was never good at ages—now everyone looks young. (Jaws Theme: Dum Dum Dum Dum Dum Dum) But then, it was hard to tell—him all covered up with green surgical gown and no-lip frog mask. His eyes looked young. Everyone's did. Bright-eyed, the mutant green frogs are rearing to go.

Ow, ow, ow, ow. I had an incredible urge to pee and I was back in the OR putting all my thought into not peeing in everyone's face. Fearlessly, Dr. Sawchuck looked for a long time. The Med/Surg nurse held my feet.

Well, he didn't find a tumor or whatever. He found an enlarged prostrate. They're always finding things. The wrong things. So it's back in October for microscopic . . . something.

Nobody said how much peeing would hurt after, but it's ok now which is more than I can say for the indented window jamb above the toilet. Now I sit at my desk. The mass is the same size, but don't hurt like it did. (Maybe I should take radioactive iodine more frequently.)

So I sit at my desk, the boy in me wanting to cry, the man writing:

With brain-cast shovels
And experiential rakes
I sit at my desk
Looking hard and long.
Finding nothing, but
the boy in me weeping
On the landfill of Yesterdays.
The man,

Biting hard and long,
His daily bread.
Composting screams
Into psychobabble afterthought.
Smoldering in review
Like undegradable diapers
Or immolated monks,
Won't scream.

The boy
Sitting hard and long
Would scream,
But he has not;
Fearing the man would scream
And scream away today's
Surreal reflections killing time
Across the cinder polished windows
Of his disenchanted eyes.

They sit there then,
Waiting hard and long,
The boy in the man,
On the verge of violence
The edge of God,
Suppressing screams
In the landfill of Yesterday's
Apathetic to-days,
For time to pass or God to care.

The man calmly observes—finding nothing. I decide to see Dr. Leahe
again. He is into dreams.

"Well. There was this Third World head on a piece of Styrofoam. And I knew
I was there to move this head from window-to-window so the head could see
out. Then I was holding the head and crying and crying and crying until a
disembodied voice to my left says, 'You can stop now.' And I'm all of a sudden
on top of this humped red tile circle, noticing the sand grout between the tiles
and this weird hump curvature. There's someone behind me, I (the observer)
know this, but I'm looking forward and see an area of sandy, prairie type terrain

between me and this rock-lined pool filled with real blue water. Beyond the pool is a huge rock masonry wall, all nice and sandy-warm colored feeling, that stretched high and all around. Someone? Close by thought or I picked the thought that, 'This is all yours.' 'This is all mine?' I said and woke up."

"That was my last nightmare. And so real. Like the one days before—where I woke up fumbling with my rifle and finally shooting the two strangers at the foot of my bed. Then I woke up. But most of my nightmares are the same. Empty. Wet, glistening streets around three in the morning, muted gunfire, the horizon flashing silently. So lonely. Why is there no one in my dreams?"

"Have you ever been shot at?" Dr. Leahe asks.

"Yes."

"Well?", he responds, "What was your MOS?"

"I was an explosives specialist, worked with napalm, CBUs, antipersonnel mines, recovered bombs, whatever . . . a moral blasphemy, according to Dr. Martin Luther King and the Southeast Asia Times, as most of the victims were woman and children. Did you ever hear what a 'psychosocial' target was? Hospitals, clinics and schools, that's what they were."

"Well?" Dr. Leahe says, "What would you expect?"

"Well, I guess I'm normal then, huh?"

"Yep", the good doctor says.

The next good doctor in Med/Surg says, "I don't want to discharge you because you'll never get back in."

"That's a crock-of-shit", I respond, thinking I earned access here by signing off six years of primetime living. Plus it's your freaking chemicals you're worried about.

"I don't want to hear this", the doctor exits. And comes back in five minutes with more blood work orders and an appointment for April. Like nothing happened.

"Check in if your pee turns to coke or you have a pain in your leg or back—otherwise, I'll see you in April."

I assumed this year. I didn't ask, but I waited. I didn't go back until they scraped me off the jailhouse floor. BP 186/120 or something. I almost died again.

THE GAINESVILLE VA
MEDICAL CENTER

They won't talk about it when asked what they feel dropping bombs on apartment buildings. "A slight bump to the wing" is all you'll get. They won't talk about the wounded Iraqis tagged "Range Balls", because who talks about losing golf balls on the Driving Range? They don't talk about PTSD preferring "Adjustment Disorder" or "Family Problems" for their lack of compensation. They won't talk about children killed in cross-fire get one tenth the market value of a Toyota run over by a tank. They won't talk about the one thousand attempted suicides per month under VA care. They won't talk about the eighteen veterans who "off" themselves daily, four of them from the Mid East. They won't talk about fighting wars by skimping on compensation as a tried-and-true strategy. They won't talk about Pfc. Jason Scheverman who decided to step in a closet shooting himself to find some peace. They won't talk about overmedicating and understating the scope of the problem. They won't talk about the number of suicides exceeding the number of combat deaths. They won't even talk about still standing in the way of veterans struggling with Agent Orange exposure.

Who gives a shit anyway? Talk's cheap.

When I walked into the clinic and saw a surgeon sitting there, I knew the biopsy wasn't benign, prompting the thought, 'God gives us pain so death won't be a disappointment.' A comforting thought don't you think? The doctor begins, "Did you bring any family members?" The doctor is sitting there as if I am the last in a long line of pathology reports and takes my "No" silently as he grabs for some papers. He must be thinking, 'We are all going to die too maybe' and reads the report in monotone, ending, ... GL 5+4=9. Do you know what that is?"

I do now. Veterans exposed to Agent Orange have much greater risks of getting the most aggressive forms of cancer (Gleason scale 8-10) than those not exposed. I feel closer to Spencer the Dog, now that we have possibly the same amount of time left.

"I'd get surgery soon, because if you do radiation first and the cancer comes back, it makes surgery harder later or you can do Watchful Wait," the surgeon finishes.

Wait for a metastatic explosion? I waited until the kids beat my avoidance to submission a few months later and choose targeted radiation, but before leaving asked, "Why did you want to know about my family?" And he says, "Because I didn't want to have to repeat myself." Assuming, I guess, I would faint after his dissertation, my laymen brain having been overloaded. Seeing me still upright and not in shock must have made his day, but he never smiled.

Since then, a hyperactive series of tests and measurements, providing the illusion of progress, revealed Ischemic Heart Disease associated with Agent Orange, profound bilateral frontal lobe atrophy, a Left Ventricle conduction delay, paradoxical wall movement, service-connected Anxiety Disorder, panic attacks, and Psychiatry opining, ... that the inherently stressful nature (of my) military work and location is scientifically documented to expose and result in PTSD" and . . . . as a result of the ongoing nature of Mr. Dewey's service, research documents that this chronic exposure experienced in the military is more disabling than PTSD following acute onset triggers."

All of which prompted the examining physician to "Advise clinical correlation" of the whole mess. Which, translated by a private physician for $65, meant—"What The Fuck!" (WTF).

"NOTES ON AN ALUMINUM CAN"

Did you know that high levels of Aluminum have been associated with the brain pathology in Alzheimer's disease? I'm a little confused. Why are we saving Aluminum cans? I mean, you would think we'd be a far cry from Aluminum, being associated with Alzheimer's and all. Actually, I personally was never this confused before the Aluminum can.

Thank you for the printed word. One theory proposes that the Roman Empire ultimately died of Plumbism (Lead Poisoning). Their lead pipes and vessels a monument to Right Brain visions and Left Brain optimism. They were up to their brains in lead. Like being knee-deep in Aluminum cans.

Industrial man has Aluminum cans. Well, there's more testimony to Man's ingenuity than Aluminum cans; but what the hey, I'm not here to bash the Right Brain. It's Aluminum I want to examine. Like why do we save it? Aluminum is the most common element found in the Earth's crust. Common as dirt. We side our houses in it. Cook in it. The properties of Aluminum seduce the Right Brain. Aluminum is everywhere! (I personally witnessed Aluminum while writing "Kilroy" on a Tunisian wall, but that's another story.)

Think of it. Aluminum. Aluminum. Everywhere. Natural, but kind of disquieting never the less, don't you think? Aluminum. Alzheimer's. Everywhere. An insidious relationship. Like Lead Poisoning . . . perhaps suggesting that Nature's abundance of Aluminum has been orchestrated, just in case Lead didn't work. :(

So why do we save Aluminum cans? Politicians don't drink from them.

"ON HAVING A PSYCHIATRIC PROBLEM IN THE 20th CENTURY"

> Do not believe anything on the mere authority of teachers or priests.
> Accept as true and as the guide to your life only that which accords
> with your own reason and experience.—Buddha

In forming his beliefs, Thomas Jefferson had but one main rule—to think of principles himself and submit these principles to experience. Jefferson was a radical and had problems, no doubt, with authority. So, at face value, being told you have a problem with authority by a Veteran's Hospital psychiatrist who could not tell the difference between a mortar ("Piss tube") and a latrine wasn't too troubling—until I pondered on which authority he was speaking of. Spiritual? Secular? Rational?

If the spirit is the image of God, then that authority is Absolute truth, the Meaning to Life, our reason for Being. However, you say it, being true to this Authority for Believers would be of first order. Nor do I question the authority of Jesus on virtue or Jefferson's authority on the Bill of Rights. I wouldn't even argue with the Biologists' authority on cell division—which they termed G.O.D.—the "Generator Of Diversity" (Klein, 1992). No, after pondering, I realized there is a problem indeed and it's choosing to live with spirit and reason in a schizophrenic world governed by irrational, self-serving authority.

My collection of genes, chemicals and conditioned behaviors are supposed to be easily manipulated, as easy as a dog could be trained to salivate at the sound of a bell. I'm a social deviant, pathological, because I refuse to be manipulated and don't accept the poisonous certainties fed to us by authorities? Go figure.

Anybody with a normal everyday problem can be routinely diagnosed in psychiatry as having a "mental illness" whether there is an actual basis in reality or not. Why? Because Psychiatry is based on "faith", not evidence.

Throughout the DSM-IV (American Psychiatric Association, 1994) there are repeated affirmations of the lack of relevant empirical research findings bearing on issues concerning the construct and predictive validity of the categories (i.e., their scientific meaningfulness). DSM-IV consists largely of categories that have been introduced and retained, not on the basis of science, but on the basis of political consensus unconstrained by empirical research. The kid who fidgets is hyperactive or suffers from attention deficit disorder. (Over a million kids are currently on the government approved addictive amphetamine Ritalin, while simultaneously are being saved from drugs by the War on "some" Drugs.) Migraine suffers have a "pain disorder", low math scores get a "developmental arithmetic disorder", if you have poor composition or organization of written text you have "developmental expressive writing disorder", arguing with your parent's gets you "oppositional defiance disorder", and even a toddler who likes "Twinkies" over Gerber's spinach has a "feeding disorder" if continued over a period of time. Hello.

Why is the world schizophrenic and not me, you ask? Well, in a psychiatric sense, there are disturbances in emotional, behavioral and intellectual functioning here, ha ha; but hold the thorazine, prolixin, haldol, or whatever else the Government has up it's sleeve—there is no withdrawal from reality, no fragmentation, and no progressive deterioration as is evident in the world body. In a religious sense, the human spirit simply cannot split into fragments as our institutions, bureaucracies and culture has. This existential truth was known even to schizophrenics long before 20th Century psychiatry stumbled into it.

Believe me I've chosen to withdraw, but unfortunately reality Is everything that remains after wishing the bad stuff away. I've tried to fragment my spiritual self with Orwellian distinctions, to split the Meaning of Life from the meaning to Daily Living in a calculated, technically well-managed way (May, 1958) toward some kind of amnesia. Education, work, home schooling, family. Well, I tried. Schizophrenia just isn't within my power.

In contrast, the World, as defined by irrational authorities, has sophisticated mechanisms for withdrawal. A 20th Century Mark Twain would call most, "Denials, damn denials, and statistics." Smoke and mirrors in the vernacular. Cruder methods developed by Goebbels simply bludgeon you with lies until they become truths and as we can see—who needs sophistication?

Then we have the separation of Church and State—which is good, but Jefferson never intended for the values of each to be separate. (I sure wish I could compartmentalize. It must be convenient.) E.G. Witness our whole economy based on interest in complete disobeyence of what Moses, Aristotle and the great Christian teachers of the Middle Ages taught. Reaping what hasn't been sown is now described as interest or investment and is defined by law, not moral teaching.

According to Gross (1998) in The End of Sanity, "blatantly irrational behavior is rapidly being established as the norm in almost every area of human endeavor." (This is not stunning news as Swift once observed that "Man is not a rational creature, he is only capable of reason.") Gross continued, "Americans know something without a name is undermining the nation, turning the mind mushy when it comes to separating truth from falsehood and right from wrong." Given this Wonderland climate, how does one guide a family without sacrificing sanity or spirit to one authority or another? How do you define, what is "due" Caesar or the Queen of Hearts for your children or yourself? From where do you choose a path, your coping strategies and therapies?

Buddha was a rich man and his family fully grown before he became a great teacher who taught detachment from worldly things. Easy for him. The greatest teacher of all, Jesus, never married, while enjoining us to "live like the birds". The great visionaries literally came out of the deserts—alone. None made choosing easy. All made their choices without the troublesome responsibility of family. None surrendered their choices to family or group, no doubt prompting Jefferson to write, "If I could not go to Heaven but with a party, I would not go there at all."

The paraphrase, "If we let the government decide what foods we eat, and what medicines we take, our bodies will soon be in a sorry state as are the souls of those who live under tyranny", has been widely attributed to Jefferson who exactly wrote, "Was the government to prescribe to us our medicine and diet, our bodies would be in such keeping as our souls are now." (Jefferson, 1792). The concept remains the same. I.E. Choice must be individual. It can't be Caesar's choice and God doesn't want it.

Well, I've searched the coping strategies toward alleviating the pain in my existence and found in the psychiatric literature that the single-most, therapeutic substance known to 20th Century man living in a schizophrenic world is marijuana. As an herb, it is arguably the least toxic substance in man's pharmacopoeia of psychoactives (Young, 1988). Why is it then, that the government prescribes chemicals with page length adverse reactions in lieu of it? I'm not sure where physicians find their truth in between the Hippocratic Oath, their patient's well being and an irrational State. I've found my truths in Genesis 1:29 and the pudding of coping strategies.

How can you as an individual responsible for your own existence, survive against this pervasive subjugation of your soul by government and religious institutions with their certainties and choices engraved in tomes and on stones? Simply disobey.

So I now have a problem with irrational authority and I'm on my way to court again. But on the way I grieve for you, my brothers and sisters, as schizophrenic lifestyles and neurotic conformity are just as problematic and painfully anxious as the angst arising from the freedom to choose for yourself.

REFS

American Psychiatric Association. Diagnostic and Statistical Manual of Mental Disorders. 4th ed. (DSM-IV). Washington, D.C.: APA. 1994.

Gross, Martin L. The End of Sanity: Social and Cultural Madness in America. Harper Perennial.1998.

Jefferson, Thomas. Notes on Virginia Q.XVII, 1782. ME 2:222. 1792.

Klein, George. "Biological Individuality". MD July 1992, 83-92.

May, Rollo. The Existential Approach. IN: Handbook of Psychiatry: Volume Two. New York: Basic Books. 1959.

Young, Andrew. "Administrative Judge Urges Medicinal Use of Marijuana" Washington Post, September 7, 1988, p.42

www.ingramcontent.com/pod-product-compliance
Lightning Source LLC
Chambersburg PA
CBHW031253280526
45784CB00004B/1831